Engineering Science Experiments

EXPERIMENTS FOR FUTURE SCIENTISTS

Engineering Science Experiments

Edited by Aviva Ebner, Ph.D.

CHELSEA HOUSE
An Infobase Learning Company

ENGINEERING SCIENCE EXPERIMENTS

Chelsea House
An imprint of Infobase Learning
132 West 31st Street
New York NY 10001

Library of Congress Cataloging-in-Publication Data
Engineering science experiments/edited by Aviva Ebner.
    p.cm.—(Experiments for future scientists)
Includes bibliographical references and index.
ISBN 978-1-60413-852-8 (alk. paper)
1. Engineering—Experiments—Juvenile literature. 2. Civil engineering—Experiments—Juvenile literature. 3. Physics—Experiments—Juvenile literature. I. Ebner, Aviva. II. Title. III. Series.
TA149.E54 2011
620.0078—dc22

                          2010029121

Chelsea House books are available at special discounts when purchased in bulk quantities for businesses, associations, institutions, or sales promotions. Please call our Special Sales Department in New York at (212) 967-8800 or (800) 322-8755.

You can find Chelsea House on the World Wide Web at http://www.infobasepublishing.com

All links and Web addresses were checked and verified to be correct at the time of publication. Because of the dynamic nature of the Web, some addresses and links may have changed since publication and may no longer be valid.

Editor: Frank K. Darmstadt
Copy Editor for A Good Thing, Inc.: Milton Horowitz
Project Coordination: Aaron Richman
Art Director: Howard Petlack
Production: Shoshana Feinstein
Illustrations: Hadel Studios
Cover printed by: Yurchak Printing, Landisville, Pa.
Book printed and bound by: Yurchak Printing, Landisville, Pa.
Date printed: June 2011
Printed in the United States of America

10 9 8 7 6 5 4 3 2 1

This book is printed on acid-free paper.

Contents

Preface

Educational representatives from several states have been meeting to come to an agreement about common content standards. Because of the No Child Left Behind Act, there has been a huge push in each individual state to teach to the standards. Teacher preparation programs have been focusing on lesson plans that are standards-based. Teacher evaluations hinge on evidence of such instruction, and various districts have been discussing merit pay for teachers linked to standardized test scores.

The focus in education has shifted to academic content rather than to the learner. In the race to raise test scores, some schools no longer address all areas of a well-rounded education and have cut elective programs completely. Also, with "high-stakes" standardized testing, schools must demonstrate a constant increase in student achievement to avoid the risk of being taken over by another agency or labeled by it as failing. The appreciation of different talents among students is dwindling; a one-size-fits-all mentality has taken its place. While innovative educators struggle to teach the whole child and recognize that each student has his or her own strengths, teachers are still forced to teach to the test. Perhaps increasing test scores helps close the gap between schools. However, are we creating a generation of students not prepared for the variety of careers available to them? Many students have not had a fine-arts class, let alone been exposed to different fields in science. We *must* start using appropriate strategies for helping all students learn to the best of their abilities. The first step in doing this is igniting a spark of interest in a child.

Experiments for Future Scientists is a six-volume series designed to expose students to various fields of study in grades five to eight (though many of the experiments can be easily adapted to lower elementary or high school level), which are the formative middle school years when students are eager to explore the world around them. Each volume focuses on a different scientific discipline and alludes to possible careers or fields of study related to those disciplines. Each volume contains 20 experiments with a detailed introduction, a step-by-step experiment that can be done in a classroom or at home, thought-provoking questions, and suggested Further Reading sources to stimulate the eager student. Of course, Safety Guidelines are provided, as well as Tips for Teachers who implement the lessons. A Scope and Sequence Chart and lists for Grade Level and Setting help the teacher with alignment to content standards, while the experiments themselves help students and adults think outside the paradigm of typical activities used in most science programs.

Science is best learned by "doing." Hands-on activities and experiments are essential, not only for grasping the concepts but also for generating excitement in today's youth. In a world of video games, benchmark tests, and fewer course choices, the experiments in these books will bring student interest back to learning. The goal is to open a child's eyes to the wonders of science and perhaps imbue some "fun" that will inspire him or her to pursue a future in a field of science. Perhaps this series will inspire some students to become future scientists.

— Aviva Ebner, Ph.D.
Faculty, University of Phoenix Online;
Faculty, Brandman University; and
Educational Consultant/Administrator K-12
Granada Hills, California

Acknowledgments

I thank the following people for their assistance and contributions to this book: Mindy Perris, science education expert, New York City Board of Education District 24, for her suggestions and samples of experiments; Janet Balekian, administrator/science educator of SIAtech schools in Los Angeles, for experiment suggestions; Boris Sinofsky, retired Los Angeles Unified School District science teacher and mentor, for his evaluation of experiments; Dr. Esther Sinofsky, Director of Instructional Media Services for Los Angeles Unified School District, for assisting with research; Michael Miller, educator, and Cassandra Ebner, college student, for their help with the glossary and index; Aaron Richman of A Good Thing, Inc., for his publishing services, along with Milton Horowitz for always providing support and a personal touch to any project; and Frank K. Darmstadt, executive editor, Chelsea House, for his consistent hard work and his confidence in me.

This book is dedicated to the memory of Faye Sinofsky, dedicated librarian and educator. She always gained joy from helping others. May we all follow her example.

Introduction

"Scientists investigate that which already is. Engineers create that which has never been."

—Albert Einstein

The Seven Wonders of the Ancient World included such amazing structures as the Great Pyramid of Giza, built as a tomb for Pharaoh Khufu; the Hanging Gardens of Babylon, multileveled gardening complete with machinery for watering the foliage; and the Lighthouse of Alexandria, which for centuries stood as one of the tallest man-made structures on Earth. Over the centuries, the list of "wonders" changed and sometimes included the Colosseum, the largest amphitheater built in the Roman Empire, and the Great Wall of China, built to protect the Chinese Empire. Modern wonders include the Empire State Building, the tallest structure in the world until 1967; the Golden Gate Bridge, one of the longest suspension bridges ever built; and the Panama Canal, that joins the Atlantic and Pacific Oceans. What do these all have in common? They are all a result of engineering.

Engineering is the profession, or often the art, of applied science, mathematics, and technology for the purpose of designing a wide variety of structures. These include materials, processes, and machines. There are several disciplines within engineering. Engineers may choose to specialize in aerospace engineering, chemical engineering, civil engineering, electrical engineering, mechanical engineering, petroleum engineering, computer engineering, genetic engineering, software engineering, nanotechnology, and molecular engineering—and new fields within engineering will continue to develop as technology advances.

Engineering Science Experiments is one book of a six-volume series exploring specific areas of the sciences to encourage students to pursue an interest in science or perhaps even plan on a career in the discipline. In "Investigating What Engineers Do," students will have the opportunity to find out what engineers in different branches of engineering do, as well as what preparation is required to pursue such a career. They will also learn about the beauty and practical function of engineering designs in

"Building and Testing a Suspension Bridge" and "Using Arches to Design and Construct a Tunnel." Students can test their skills at "Building an Earthquake-Proof Structure," "Designing a Parachute," "Creating a Full-Size Hovercraft," which floats on air, "Building an Igloo," by making a model igloo and exploring the dome structure, and "Building a Model Skyscraper," by making a model building and testing its ability to hold weight and handle wind shear. In addition, students can test already engineered items for effectiveness, such as "Testing the Durability of Different Building Materials" and "Testing the Effectiveness of Sound Barriers."

Introductory paragraphs begin each experiment. Terms shown in italics in these paragraphs are listed in the glossary. At the end of each experiment is a "Further Reading" list of references to satisfy inquisitive students.

There are many more experiments in this volume that will allow children to build, explore, test, question, and design. The idea is to spark an interest and curiosity that might one day lead to the creation of the latest wonder of the world. In the words of Walt Streightiff, an American author, "There are no seven wonders of the world in the eyes of a child. There are seven million." It is our job as educators, parents, and mentors to open their eyes and see the wonder.

Safety Guidelines

REVIEW BEFORE STARTING ANY EXPERIMENT

Each experiment includes special safety precautions that are relevant to that particular project. These do not include all the basic safety precautions that are necessary whenever you are working on a scientific experiment. For this reason, it is absolutely necessary that you read and remain mindful of the General Safety Precautions that follow. Experimental science can be dangerous and good laboratory procedure always includes following basic safety rules. Things can happen quickly while you are performing an experiment—for example, materials can spill, break, or even catch on fire. There will not be time after the fact to protect yourself. Always prepare for unexpected dangers by following the basic safety guidelines during the entire experiment, whether or not something seems dangerous to you at a given moment.

We have been quite sparing in prescribing safety precautions for the individual experiments. For one reason, we want you to take very seriously the safety precautions that are printed in this book. If you see it written here, you can be sure that it is here because it is absolutely critical.

Read the safety precautions here and at the beginning of each experiment before performing each lab activity. It is difficult to remember a long set of general rules. By rereading these general precautions every time you set up an experiment, you will be reminding yourself that lab safety is critically important. In addition, use your good judgment and pay close attention when performing potentially dangerous procedures. Just because the book does not say "Be careful with hot liquids" or "Don't cut yourself with a knife" does not mean that you can be careless when boiling water or using a knife to punch holes in plastic bottles. Notes in the text are special precautions to which you must pay special attention.

GENERAL SAFETY PRECAUTIONS

Accidents can be caused by carelessness, haste, or insufficient knowledge. By practicing safety procedures and being alert while conducting experiments, you can avoid taking an unnecessary risk. Be sure to check the individual experiments in this book for additional safety regulations and adult supervision requirements. If you will be working in a laboratory, do not work alone. When you are working off site, keep in groups with a minimum of three students per group, and follow school rules and state legal requirements for the number of supervisors required. Ask an adult supervisor with basic training in first aid to carry a small first-aid kit. Make sure everyone knows where this person will be during the experiment.

PREPARING

- Clear all surfaces before beginning experiments.
- Read the entire experiment before you start.
- Know the hazards of the experiments and anticipate dangers.

PROTECTING YOURSELF

- Follow the directions step by step.
- Perform only one experiment at a time.
- Locate exits, fire blanket and extinguisher, master gas and electricity shut-offs, eyewash, and first-aid kit.
- Make sure there is adequate ventilation.
- Do not participate in horseplay.
- Do not wear open-toed shoes.
- Keep floor and workspace neat, clean, and dry.
- Clean up spills immediately.
- If glassware breaks, do not clean it up by yourself; ask for teacher assistance.
- Tie back long hair.
- Never eat, drink, or smoke in the laboratory or workspace.
- Do not eat or drink any substances tested unless expressly permitted to do so by a knowledgeable adult.

USING EQUIPMENT WITH CARE

- Set up apparatus far from the edge of the desk.
- Use knives or other sharp, pointed instruments with care.

- Pull plugs, not cords, when removing electrical plugs.
- Clean glassware before and after use.
- Check glassware for scratches, cracks, and sharp edges.
- Let your teacher know about broken glassware immediately.
- Do not use reflected sunlight to illuminate your microscope.
- Do not touch metal conductors.
- Take care when working with any form of electricity.
- Use alcohol-filled thermometers, not mercury-filled thermometers.

USING CHEMICALS

- Never taste or inhale chemicals.
- Label all bottles and apparatus containing chemicals.
- Read labels carefully.
- Avoid chemical contact with skin and eyes (wear safety glasses or goggles, lab apron, and gloves).
- Do not touch chemical solutions.
- Wash hands before and after using solutions.
- Wipe up spills thoroughly.

HEATING SUBSTANCES

- Wear safety glasses or goggles, apron, and gloves when heating materials.
- Keep your face away from test tubes and beakers.
- When heating substances in a test tube, avoid pointing the top of the test tube toward other people.
- Use test tubes, beakers, and other glassware made of Pyrex™ glass.
- Never leave apparatus unattended.
- Use safety tongs and heat-resistant gloves.
- If your laboratory does not have heatproof workbenches, put your Bunsen burner on a heatproof mat before lighting it.
- Take care when lighting your Bunsen burner; light it with the airhole closed and use a Bunsen burner lighter rather than wooden matches.

- Turn off hot plates, Bunsen burners, and gas when you are done.
- Keep flammable substances away from flames and other sources of heat.
- Have a fire extinguisher on hand.

FINISHING UP

- Thoroughly clean your work area and any glassware used.
- Wash your hands.
- Be careful not to return chemicals or contaminated reagents to the wrong containers.
- Do not dispose of materials in the sink unless instructed to do so.
- Clean up all residues and put in proper containers for disposal.
- Dispose of all chemicals according to all local, state, and federal laws.

BE SAFETY CONSCIOUS AT ALL TIMES!

1. INVESTIGATING WHAT ENGINEERS DO

Introduction

Engineering is a profession that applies scientific and mathematical knowledge to designing structures, machines, and other objects or systems. There are different types of *engineers*, including professional engineers, chartered engineers, and incorporated engineers. Those engineers licensed for a specific subject area focus on a special field of application. Although there have been many recent technological advances—thanks to engineers—engineering has existed since ancient times. When you study the pyramids of Egypt or the *aqueducts* of Rome, it becomes clear that these structures were designed by engineers of those time periods. Inventions throughout history have applied technology. Today, we have several different fields of engineering including acoustical, *aerospace*, chemical, civil, electrical, and mechanical engineering.

In this activity, you will research what engineers do, the history of engineering, what type of education prepares people for engineering, and careers in engineering.

Time Needed

3 to 4 days to research, 3 to 4 hours to complete

What You Need

- ✎ computer with Internet access or access to a library
- ✎ access to a university that has an engineering program (e.g., ability to visit in person or correspond via e-mail, regular mail, or telephone)

✎   paper

✎   pen

✎   glue stick

✎   scissors

✎   stapler

✎   printer (if using a computer)

 ## Safety Precautions

Please review and follow the safety guidelines at the beginning of this volume. Always exercise caution when accessing the Internet, and follow all Internet safety guidelines. Get permission from your parents to correspond with others.

What You Do

1. Using the Internet or a library, research what an engineer does. Make sure to keep track of your sources. Try to gather information about the following questions:

   a. What is an engineer?

   b. What is the history of the field of engineering?

   c. Who were among the first engineers?

   d. What are the different fields of specialization in engineering?

   e. What does each type of engineer do?

   f. What are some everyday items, objects, or activities we would not have if it were not for engineers?

   g. If possible, print out some photographs of some of these items or activities.

2. Contact the engineering department of a university and find out what the requirements are to be accepted in the program and what the requirements are to complete a degree in engineering.

(For example, what coursework must be taken?) You can look up information via the Internet. Some suggested URLs include http://www.engineer.ucla.edu/, http://www.caltech.edu/, and http://web.mit.edu/. However, you are encouraged to visit a local university or contact one near you. Also find out what careers are available to engineers. Use the data table as a guide.

3. Create an information packet on engineering using the information you collected.

   a. Prepare a cover page using some of the illustrations you printed (Figure 1). Be sure to include a title and your name.

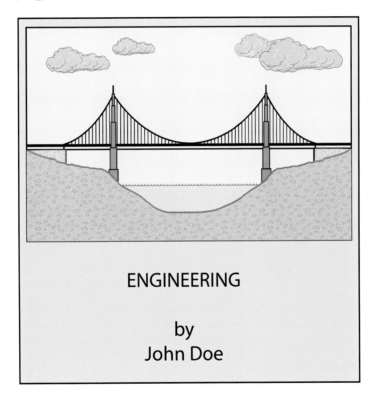

Figure 1

   b. Create a table of contents with the following chapters: What Is an Engineer?, History of Engineering, Fields in Engineering, How Engineering Has Benefited Us, How to Become an Engineer, Careers in Engineering, and References.

   c. Whenever possible, include photos printed from your sources.

Data Table		
Required subject	Requirements for entry in an engineering program	Requirements for completion of an engineering degree
English		
Math		
Science		
Social studies		
Foreign language		
Visual or performing arts		
Other		

 Observations

1. Did you learn anything new about what engineers do?
2. List one item you use on a regular basis that you did not realize was made by an engineer. What would your life be like without that item?
3. Which careers in engineering interest you the most? Why?

Our Findings

Please refer to the Our Findings appendix at the back of this volume.

Further Reading

"California Institute of Technology." CalTech. 2009. Available online. URL: http://www.caltech.edu/. Accessed December 17, 2009. Information Web site for CalTech, a top-rated West Coast college for engineering.

Douglas, David, Greg Papadoupolis, and John Boutelle. *Citizen Engineer: A Handbook for Socially Responsible Engineering*. Upper Saddle River, NJ: Prentice Hall, 2009. Explains what an engineer must take into account when designing projects, including the impact on the environment and society.

"Engineering." *The Columbia Encyclopedia*, 6th ed. 2008. Available online. URL: http://www.encyclopedia.com. Accessed December 17, 2009. Article about several fields within engineering.

"Massachusetts Institute of Technology." MIT. 2009. Available online. URL: http://web.mit.edu/. Accessed December 17, 2009. Informational Web site for MIT, a top-rated East Coast college for engineering.

Petroski, Henry. *Remaking the World: Adventures in Engineering*. New York: Vintage, 1998. Discusses how engineers are responsible for world development because of the impact of their contributions.

Selinger, Carl. *Stuff You Don't Learn in Engineering School: Skills for Success in the Real World*. Hoboken, NJ: Wiley, 2004. Includes information about time management, business, and decision making in the world of engineering.

2. BUILDING A LAUNCHER/CATAPULT

Introduction

A *catapult* is a machine used to launch *projectiles*. In ancient and *medieval* times, catapults were used in warfare. Early versions in ancient times were used to launch arrows. Later, in order to invade medieval castles and walled cities, catapults were necessary in *sieges*, with fiery projectiles launched over the castle walls. After the *advent* of gunpowder, catapults were replaced by cannons. However, in even more modern times, catapults were used to propel *grenades* during World War I. Today, variations of the catapult are used to launch *torpedoes* from ships and to assist aircraft in taking off from *sea carriers* with short runways.

Catapults can be made easily from common materials. They can be built in a variety of sizes, but all are based on the idea of being able to use a small amount of force to propel an object with a greater force than could be accomplished without the device.

In this activity, you will build a small catapult and use it to launch objects.

Time Needed

1 to 2 hours to make, 20 minutes to complete

What You Need

- large craft stick
- lid from a baby food jar
- large wooden clothespin

✎   glue

✎   2 pieces of wood, one about 3 inches (in.) by 3 in. (7.5 centimeters [cm] by 7.5 cm) and the other a small plank about a foot long (about 30 cm)

✎   10 marshmallows

✎   measuring tape

Safety Precautions

Please review and follow the safety guidelines at the beginning of this volume.

What You Do

1. Glue the clothespin to the plank of wood (Figure 1).

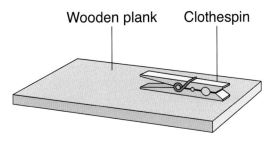

Wooden plank   Clothespin

Figure 1

2. Glue the small block of wood on top of the raised end of the clothespin (Figure 2).

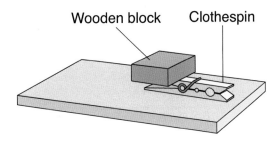

Wooden block   Clothespin

Figure 2

3. Allow the items in steps 1 and 2 to dry.

4. Glue the lid of the baby food jar to the end of the large craft stick (Figure 3).

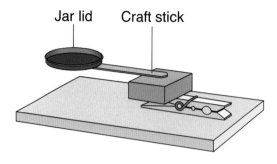

Figure 3

5. Let glue on the lid and stick to dry.

6. Glue the large craft stick over the small block of wood as shown in Figure 4.

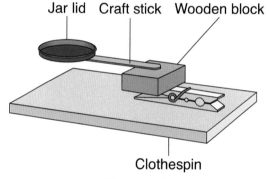

Figure 4

7. Let the glue dry.

8. Place a marshmallow in the lid (Figure 5).

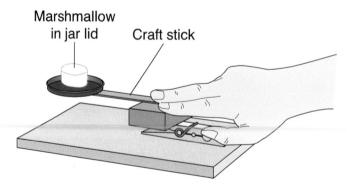

Figure 5

9. Push down on the craft stick where it is glued to the block so that the clothespin is compressed (Figure 5).

10. Let go so that the clothespin opens, and watch the marshmallow fly.

11. Measure how far away the marshmallow landed from the catapult.

12. Record the measurements on the data table.

13. With the rest of the marshmallows, repeat steps 8 to 12, a total of 9 more times.

Data Table	
Marshmallow	**Distance**
1	
2	
3	
4	
5	
6	
7	
8	
9	
10	

 **Observations**

1. Calculate the average distance your marshmallows were propelled by the catapult. (Add all your measurements and divide by 10.)
2. What modifications could you make to the device to be able to launch the marshmallows even farther?
3. What simple machine is the basis for this catapult?
4. Sketch some other designs for creating a catapult or launcher using other materials.

Our Findings

Please refer to the Our Findings appendix at the back of this volume. Do not launch any hard objects from the catapult; doing so may cause harm to anyone who is hit.

Further Reading

"Castle." *The Columbia Encyclopedia*, 6th ed. 2008. Available online. URL: http://www.encyclopedia.com/doc/1E1-castle.html. Accessed December 26, 2009. Encyclopedia entry on the different types of castles built throughout history.

"Catapult." *The Columbia Encyclopedia*, 6th ed. 2008. Available online. URL: http://www.encyclopedia.com/doc/1E1-catapult.html. Accessed December 26, 2009. Explains the use of the launcher in ancient and medieval times.

Catapults.info. "What Is a Catapult?" Available online. URL: http://www.catapults.info/. Accessed October 5, 2010. This Web site explains ancient technology and discusses the use of the catapult.

Gravett, Christopher. *The History of Castles: Fortifications Around the World.* Guilford, CT: Lyons Press, 2001. Illustrated with photographs and maps, provides a visual tour of famous castles around the world.

Medieval-Castle-Siege-Weapons.com. "Building Catapults Required Engineering Know How." Available online. URL: http://www.medieval-castle-siege-weapons.com/building-catapults.html. Accessed October 5, 2010. This Web site about medieval weapons discusses the role played by engineers in ancient times and what was needed to build a catapult on site.

PBS.org. "Secrets of Lost Empires." Available online. URL: http://www.pbs.org/wgbh/nova/lostempires/trebuchet/. Accessed October 5, 2010. Site for the PBS show NOVA that includes a slide show on a catapult that was built.

Rihll, Tracey. *Catapult: A History.* Chicago: Westholme Publishing, 2007. Illustrated with drawings and photographs, details the history and uses of the catapult.

"Siege." *The Columbia Encyclopedia*, 6th ed. 2008. Available online. URL: http://www.encyclopedia.com/doc/1E1-siege.html. Accessed December 26, 2009. Encyclopedia entry detailing how a siege worked as a strategy of warfare.

Whipps, Heather. "Catapults Invented Before Theory Explained Them." October 9, 2007. Available online. URL: http://www.livescience.com/history/071009-first-catapult.html. Accessed October 5, 2010. The article claims that ancient civilizations did not need advanced math to figure out how to make a simple catapult.

3. BUILDING AND TESTING A SUSPENSION BRIDGE

Introduction

Suspension bridges are designed with the *load*-carrying portion or deck hanging below suspension *cables*. Suspension bridges, compared to some other kinds of bridges, allow for a greater load to be carried across the bridge. The ends of the cables must be *anchored* in place so that the *tension* in the cables can support the extra load. The other forces involved in a suspension bridge include *compression* in the *pillars* or towers. All of these forces allow for suspension bridges to *span* longer distances than other types of bridges and, if built accordingly, be able to better withstand earthquakes. However, engineers must also design suspension bridges so that they do not sway a lot in the wind. Well-known suspension bridges include the Brooklyn Bridge in New York City and the Golden Gate Bridge in San Francisco.

In this experiment, you will build a simple suspension bridge and test its load capacity.

Time Needed

1 hour

What You Need

- 7 straws
- 4 large paper clips
- dental floss
- masking tape

- scissors
- small paper cup
- pennies
- ruler
- 2 tables
- 2 chairs with straight backs
- paper, 1 sheet
- pen or pencil

Safety Precautions

Please review and follow the safety guidelines at the beginning of this volume.

What You Do

1. Cut 2 short pieces from 1 straw, each about 1.25 inches (in.) (3 centimeters [cm]) long.

2. Tape 2 long straws to 1 short piece of straw (Figure 1).

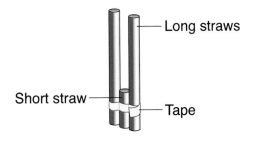

Short straw — Long straws
— Tape

Figure 1

3. Tape together the 2 long straws at the top (Figure 2).

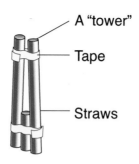

Figure 2

4. Repeat steps 2 and 3. These will be the 2 towers for your bridge.

5. Tape each tower to the end of a table (Figure 3).

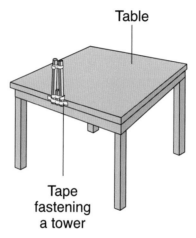

Figure 3

6. Partially unbend 1 paper clip (Figure 4).

Figure 4

7. Poke the paper clip's ends through the upper portion of the paper cup (Figure 5).

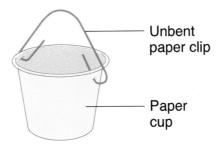

Figure 5

8. Attach the middle of the paper clip to another paper clip (Figure 6).

Figure 6

9. Move the 2 tables so that they are about 7 in. (17 cm) apart.

10. Slide a straw through the paper clip that is attached to the cup/ paper clip assembly (Figure 7).

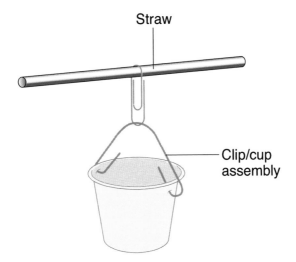

Figure 7

11. Place the long straw so that it rests on the short straw of each of 2 towers (Figure 8). This represents a beam bridge.

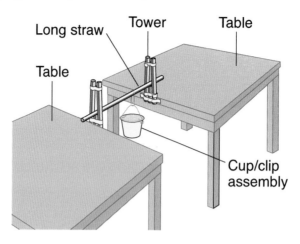

Figure 8

12. Add pennies to the cup until the straw bends. This is called a load test.

13. Record the number of pennies you added.

14. Empty the pennies from the cup.

15. Remove the straw and the paper cup assembly.

16. Place a new straw in the same place as the previous one.

17. Cut a piece of dental floss about 4 feet long (100 cm).

18. Tie the middle of the floss string to the center of the straw (Figure 9).

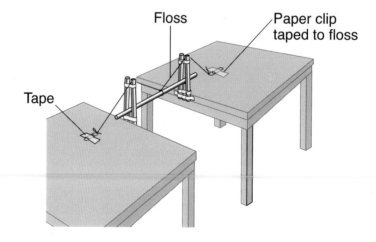

Figure 9

19. Run each end of the floss through the top of the towers, just above the tape (Figure 9).

20. Tie each end of the floss to a paper clip (Figure 9).

21. Tape down the paper clips to the tables so that the floss is taut (Figure 9).

22. Take the paper clip/paper cup assembly you made in steps 6 to 8 and attach it to the middle of the straw suspension bridge.

23. Repeat the load test by adding pennies to the cup.

24. Keep adding pennies until the straw bends.

25. Record the number of pennies you added.

 **Observations**

1. How many pennies were you able to add to the first (beam) bridge before it bent?

2. How many pennies were you able to add to the second (suspension) bridge before it bent?

3. Why do you think the suspension bridge could hold more weight?

4. What changes to your design would you make if you wanted to make the suspension bridge longer but hold the same amount of weight? What changes would you make to the design to keep it the same length but hold more weight?

Our Findings

Please refer to the Our Findings appendix at the back of this volume.

Further Reading

"Bridge." *The Columbia Encyclopedia*, 6th ed. 2008. Available online. URL: http://www.encyclopedia.com/doc/1E1-bridge-riv.html. Accessed January 1, 2010. History of and types of bridges.

"Brooklyn Bridge." *New York City Roads.* 2009. Available online. URL: http://www.nycroads.com/crossings/brooklyn/. Accessed January 1, 2010. Web site with a history of New York's Brooklyn Bridge.

Drewry, Charles Stewart. *A Memoir of Suspension Bridges.* Charleston, SC: Bibliobazaar, 2008. Detailed history of suspension bridges, including photographs.

McCullough, David. *The Great Bridge: The Epic Story of the Building of the Brooklyn Bridge.* New York: Simon & Schuster, 2001. History behind the making of the Brooklyn Bridge.

"Welcome to Golden Gate Bridge." *Golden Gate Bridge.* 2009. Available online. URL: http://www.goldengatebridge.org/. Accessed January 1, 2010. Official Web site of the Golden Gate Bridge in San Francisco, with information regarding traffic.

4. BUILDING AN EARTHQUAKE-PROOF STRUCTURE

Introduction

Civil engineering includes the planning, design, construction, and operation of our *infrastructure*, which includes roads, bridges, airports, buildings, and many other *structures*. Civil engineers have to ensure that the structures are planned and designed properly, do not go over budget in costs, are safe, serve the correct function, and, sometimes, are also *aesthetically* acceptable. One of the most important features is safety. For instance, civil engineers design structures to be *resistant to earthquakes*. No structure can be 100 percent earthquake-proof, but engineers can make buildings to withstand earthquakes by using the correct building materials and anticipating the movement of the Earth. Special structures are created within the building's *foundation*, and *reinforcement* materials are built into the walls, especially vital in areas such as California where large and frequent earthquakes occur. California has strict building codes for human safety.

In this experiment, you will create a *prototype* for an earthquake-proof structure, test it, and make changes to your design if necessary.

Time Needed

2 hours

What You Need

- 8 cardboard shoe boxes without lids
- 2 pieces of wood, each about 24 inches (in.) by 24 in. (about 60 centimeters [cm] by 60 cm)

- ✏ 6 golf balls
- ✏ 3 extra-large, heavy-duty rubber bands
- ✏ 32 small weights (metal washers can be substituted)
- ✏ 32 pipe cleaners
- ✏ 32 paperclips
- ✏ 32 toothpicks
- ✏ roll of transparent tape

Safety Precautions

Please review and follow the safety guidelines at the beginning of this volume.

What You Do

1. Place the golf balls between the 2 pieces of wood and secure the 2 pieces of wood together with the 3 rubber bands, as in Figure 1. This is your "shake table."

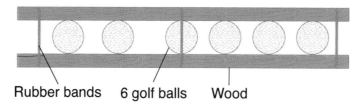

Rubber bands   6 golf balls   Wood

Figure 1

2. Test your shake table by moving the bottom piece of wood back and forth abruptly. This simulates an earthquake.

3. Stack 2 shoe boxes on their sides on top of each other on the shake table (Figure 2).

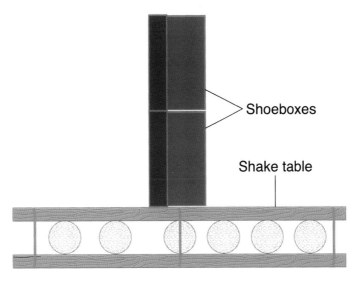

Shoeboxes

Shake table

Figure 2

4. Using the shake table, simulate an earthquake.

5. Observe if the boxes fall or remain in place.

6. Record your observations.

7. Repeat steps 3 to 6, except add another box to the top each time. Continue to do this until the boxes no longer remain standing but instead topple down when shaken.

8. Use the engineering design process to develop possible solutions to the problem of how to build a standing structure with all 8 boxes that does not fall down when shaken. However, the boxes may not be attached to each other by any means. The resources available to you are the materials you prepared for this activity.

9. Select the best possible solution out of your designs.

10. Construct a prototype by building the design out of the materials you have available.

11. Test your prototype by placing it on the shake table and shaking it.

12. Evaluate your solution.

13. If your design did not work, either try one of your other designs or redesign your original prototype (make improvements on the existing one).

 **Observations**

1. How many boxes could be stacked and still remain standing when shaken before you added the other materials?

2. Did your first prototype work; e.g., did it keep all 8 boxes from falling down when shaken?

3. Why are engineers important for the design of buildings in earthquake-prone areas?

4. What do engineers have to take into account in their designs aside from safety?

Our Findings

Please refer to the Our Findings appendix at the back of this volume.

Further Reading

Brenner, Brian. *Don't Throw This Away: The Civil Engineering Life.* Reston, VA: American Society of Civil Engineers, 2006. A funny collection of essays by an engineer on the life of a civil engineer.

"Earthquake." *The Columbia Encyclopedia*, 6th ed. 2008. Available online. URL: http://www.encyclopedia.com/doc/1E1-earthqua. html. Accessed December 27, 2009. Lengthy encyclopedia entry on earthquakes, including information on waves and plate tectonics.

Hough, Susan. *Earthshaking Science: What We Know (and Don't Know) About Earthquakes.* Princeton: Princeton University Press, 2004. Written for the non-scientific reader, explains how earthquakes occur, how they are measured, and how they impact structures.

"Plate tectonics." *The Columbia Encyclopedia*, 6th ed. 2008. Available online. URL: http://www.encyclopedia.com/doc/1E1-platetec.html. Accessed December 27, 2009. Encyclopedia entry about the field of plate tectonics, how the plates move, and the earthquakes caused by the movement.

"Seismology." *The Columbia Encyclopedia*, 6th ed. 2008. Available online. URL: http://www.encyclopedia.com/doc/1E1-seismolo.html. Accessed December 27, 2009. Lengthy article on the science of studying earthquakes, including information on the equipment used for measuring earthquakes.

5. DESIGNING A PARACHUTE

Introduction

Evidence of *parachutes* and parachute designs can be found as far back as the *Renaissance* period. Although he was not the first to sketch a parachute design, Italian artist and inventor Leonardo da Vinci (1452–1519) was among the first to draw a parachute of the appropriate proportions to support the weight of a person. Croatian inventor Faust Vrancic (1551–1617) improved on da Vinci's model. However, the modern version of the parachute was devised in 18th-century France by inventor Louis-Sebastian Lenormand (1757–1837), and the first successful jump performed with a silk parachute was done by French inventor André Garnerin (1769–1823) in 1797. Other inventors and engineers continued to improve on the design. The military eventually found the parachute a useful tool and first used it for *artillery* spotters in World War I.

There are several types of parachutes, depending on their use. Round parachutes are used to create *drag* to slow down a descending vehicle or heavy object. *Cruciform* or square parachutes are used to prevent back-and-forth movement. Ribbon parachutes are used at *sonic* speeds because a regular parachute would not work at such speeds. Finally, *ram-air parachutes,* also known as *parafoils,* are typically used now for controlling speed and direction, similar to a paraglider. No matter what the shape or use, the reason for a parachute is to slow down the speed of an object.

In this experiment, you will create several parachutes and test them for their ability to slow the rate of *descent* of an object.

Time Needed

60 minutes

What You Need

- 2 large, heavy-duty plastic garbage bags
- scissors
- ruler
- 4 twist ties
- string, 256 inches (in.) (650 centimeters [cm])
- 4 metal washers
- stopwatch
- safe, high place from which to drop parachutes (i.e., second-floor balcony, playground equipment)

Safety Precautions

Please review and follow the safety guidelines at the beginning of this volume.

What You Do

1. Cut along one side and the bottom of each plastic garbage bag so that each bag can be opened into a large plastic sheet (Figure 1).

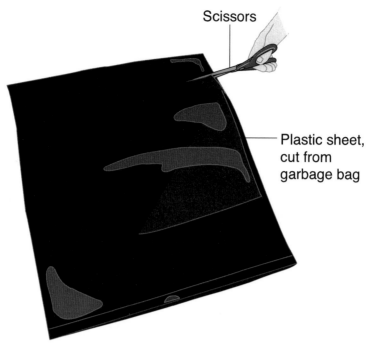

Figure 1

2. Out of the 2 bags, cut a total of 4 squares of plastic, one of each of the following sizes: about 8 in. by 8 in. (20 cm by 20 cm), about 12 in. by 12 in. (30 cm by 30 cm), about 16 in. by 16 in. (40 cm by 40 cm), and about 20 in. by 20 in. (50 cm by 50 cm).

3. At each corner of every square, tie a knot in the plastic (Figure 2).

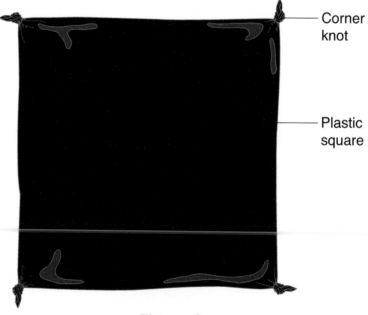

Figure 2

4. Cut the string into 16 equal pieces, each about 16 in. (40 cm) long.

5. Tie the end of each string to each corner knot of the plastic squares so that each knot has a string tied to it. Tie above the knot (Figure 3).

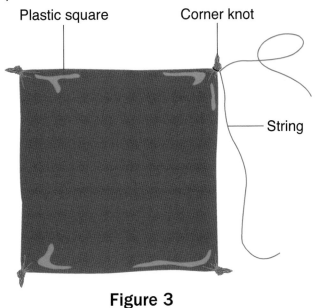

Figure 3

6. Tie into a knot the opposite ends of the 4 strings attached to each square, ensuring that the strings dangle at equal lengths to the knot (Figure 4).

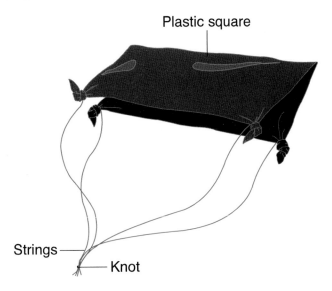

Figure 4

7. Place a twist tie through each washer (Figure 5).

Figure 5

8. Attach each washer to the end of a different set of knotted strings using the twist tie so that each of the 4 squares has a washer hanging from the end of the strings (Figure 6).

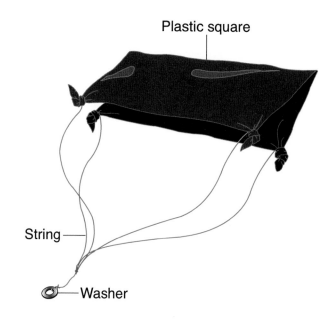

Figure 6

9. Find a safe location about 7 feet (2 meters) off the ground from which you cannot fall.

10. Hold the smallest parachute in one hand and the stopwatch in the other.

11. Start the stopwatch as soon as you let go of the parachute.

12. Stop the stopwatch as soon as the parachute hits the ground.

13. Record the time elapsed.

14. Repeat steps 10 to 13 with the other parachutes, making sure to drop each from the same height.

 **Observations**

1. Which parachute fell the fastest? Why?

2. Which parachute fell the slowest? Why?

3. Why do the parachutes fall?

4. Make a graph with time in seconds on the *X*-axis and the surface area of the parachute (square inches or square centimeters) along the *Y*-axis. What do you notice about the relationship between the surface area of the parachute and the time?

Our Findings

Please refer to the Our Findings appendix at the back of this volume.

Further Reading

Armyparatroopers.org. "Army Paratroopers—Home of the Airborne." Available online. URL: http://www.armyparatrooper.org/. Accessed October 5, 2010. A Web site for paratroopers of different generations to share experiences.

Chambers, John Whiteclay, II. "Airborne Warfare." *The Oxford Companion to American Military History*. 2000. Accessed October 5, 2010. Lengthy article on the use of airborne resources in war including paratroopers.

Germain, Brian. *The Parachute and Its Pilot: The Ultimate Guide for the Ram-Air Aviator*. Silver Spring, MD: Germain, 2004. Written by a skydiver and parachute designer with more than 10,000 jumps.

"Parachute." *The Columbia Encyclopedia*, 6th ed. 2008. Available online. URL: http://www.encyclopedia.com. Accessed December 15, 2009. Detailed entry explaining how parachutes work.

Parachutehistory.com. "Historical Review." Available online. URL: http://www.parachutehistory.com/eng/drs.html. Accessed October 5, 2010. This Web site details the history of the invention and use of parachutes.

Paratrooper.org. "Welcome to Paratrooper.org." Available online. URL: http://www.paratrooper.org/. Accessed October 5, 2010. A Web site dedicated to the 82nd Airborne Division, the first troops to parachute into France on D-Day.

Pointer, Dan. *Parachuting: The Skydiver's Handbook*. Santa Barbara, CA: Para Publishing, 2007. A comprehensive guide to skydiving for all levels of experience.

Rose, Karen. *Skydiving Handbook: Extreme Sports Guide*. Scotts Valley, CA: CreateSpace, 2009. Informational book for the layman about the sport of skydiving.

"Skydiving." *The Columbia Encyclopedia*, 6th ed. 2008. Available online. URL: http://www.encyclopedia.com. Accessed December 16, 2009. Provides a short entry on the history of skydiving.

"USPA." United States Parachute Association. Available online. URL: http://www.uspa.org/. Accessed December 15, 2009. Official Web site of the organization dedicated to safe skydiving and proper training for use of parachutes.

6. DEMONSTRATING SATELLITE ORBITS

Introduction

An *orbit* is a curved path followed by an object around another object. Johannes Kepler (1571–1630), a German mathematician and *astronomer*, is thought to be the first to state what is now known as Kepler's First Law: The orbit of a planet around the Sun will be *elliptical* in shape. A circle is essentially an *ellipse*. Depending on how far away an orbiting object is from the source of a *gravitational* pull, the object will be required to maintain a certain *velocity* to establish an elliptical orbit. Kepler was the first to successfully challenge previous beliefs that the Earth was the center of the solar system and that the planets travel in *epicycles*. Kepler's laws of planetary motion helped to establish that the planets travel at different rates of speed around the Sun. His laws are also part of the foundations of modern astronomy and physics.

In this activity, you will model orbits and adjust the velocity of an orbiting object to establish a circular orbit.

Time Needed

30 minutes

What You Need

- 1 bed sheet
- heavy-duty rope, about 3 yards (3 meters) long
- large, circular trash can
- baseball

- golf ball
- marble
- cardboard tube from inside a roll of paper towels
- scissors

Safety Precautions

Please review and follow the safety guidelines at the beginning of this volume.

What You Do

1. Stretch the sheet over the top of the open trash can.
2. With a rope, tie the sheet in place, making sure that the sheet is stretched tight (Figure 1).

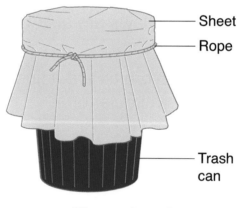

Sheet
Rope

Trash can

Figure 1

3. Set the baseball down in the middle of the stretched sheet.
4. Cut the cardboard tube lengthwise (Figure 2).

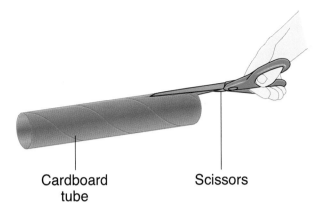

Cardboard   Scissors
tube

Figure 2

5. Using half the tube as a launcher, roll the golf ball down the tube to the edge of the circular area of the sheet over the trash can (Figure 3).

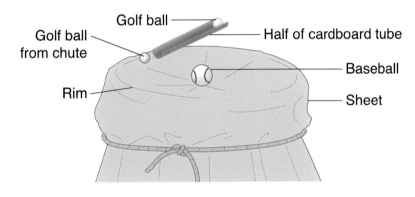

Golf ball
from chute

Golf ball ──── ── Half of cardboard tube

── Baseball

Rim ── ── Sheet

Figure 3

6. Repeat step 5, adjusting the height and angle at which you are holding the tube, until you are able to have the golf ball follow a circular orbit around the baseball.

7. Repeat steps 5 and 6 with a marble.

 **Observations**

1. Did you notice a difference in the speed of the golf ball or marble depending on the angle and height of the tube? Were you able to determine the best angle and height from which to "launch" your ball into orbit?

2. What did the baseball represent? What did the golf ball and marble represent?

3. Why do different objects travel at different speeds around the Sun?

Our Findings

Please refer to the Our Findings appendix at the back of this volume.

Further Reading

Apt, Jay, Michael Helfert, and Justin Wilkinson. *Orbit: NASA Astronauts Photograph the Earth*. Des Moines, IA: National Geographic, 2001. Photographs of the Earth taken from orbit around the Earth.

"Artificial satellite." *The Columbia Encyclopedia*, 6th ed. 2008. Available online. URL: http://www.encyclopedia.com/doc/1E1-satelart.html. Accessed January 1, 2010. Lengthy entry on what an artificial satellite is, the purpose it serves, and how it is launched into orbit.

Caspar, Max. *Kepler*. Mineola, NY: Dover Publications, 1993. Biography of the the German mathematician and astronomer Johannes Kepler.

"Johannes Kepler." *The Columbia Encyclopedia*, 6th ed. 2008. Available online. URL: http://www.encyclopedia.com/doc/1E1-Kepler-J.html. Accessed January 1, 2010. Short entry about the life of Kepler and his major contributions to science.

"Orbit." *The Columbia Encyclopedia*, 6th ed. 2008. Available online. URL: http://www.encyclopedia.com/doc/1E1-orbit.html. Accessed January 1, 2010. Detailed entry with explanations of different types of orbits.

7. BUILDING A WORKING-MODEL DAM

Introduction

Dams are *barriers* engineered to *retain* water. Dams have been built since ancient times, with evidence of dams found in times past in Mesopotamia and in the Roman Empire. Today, they are typically associated with *hydroelectric plants*, with the *water pressure* and flow used to generate *electricity*. Dams serve other purposes, too, such as *irrigation*, creating recreation areas, making a water *reservoir*, and minimizing flood risks. Dry dams are built to control flooding, while *diversionary dams* are constructed to change the course of a river. *Check dams* reduce the flow of water and help prevent severe soil *erosion*. Overflow and *saddle dams* are used to contain water. Dams can also be classified, not only according to their uses but also by their structure. Arch dams, as suggested by their name, use the arch as part of the design to strengthen the dam. *Gravity* dams are built so that their sheer weight and size prevent them from being moved. *Embankment dams* are made from pressed and compacted dirt. *Cofferdams* are used to expose an area that is usually under water, and *timber dams* were made of wood. Also, we should not leave out the beaver dam, which is constructed from mud and sticks by the beaver to flood small areas, providing food and shelter for the animal.

In this experiment, you will create one or more model dams and compare the water pressure at the top of the dam to the water pressure at the bottom of the dam.

 Time Needed

90 minutes to 2 hours

What You Need

- ✎ empty 2-liter plastic bottle
- ✎ 1 straw
- ✎ modeling clay, a small lump
- ✎ sharp scissors
- ✎ black permanent marker
- ✎ ruler, 12 inches (in.)
- ✎ funnel
- ✎ sink with running water
- ✎ pen or pencil
- ✎ 1 lined sheet of paper
- ✎ large, clear-plastic storage container
- ✎ sand, enough to fill the container
- ✎ small rocks, about 8 to 10
- ✎ craft sticks, about 20

Safety Precautions

Please review and follow the safety guidelines at the beginning of this volume.

What You Do

1. About 1 in. (about 2.5 centimeters [cm]) from the bottom of the plastic bottle, carefully poke a hole with the scissors (Figure 1).

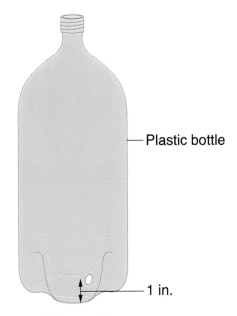

Figure 1

2. Cut off a piece of straw about 3 in. long (about 7.5 cm).

3. Insert the straw into the hole just enough so that it stays in place.

4. Mold clay around the straw where it enters the hole to keep the bottle from leaking around the edges of the hole (Figure 2).

Figure 2

5. Using the black marker, label marks on the bottle at the following distances up from the straw: 2 in. (5 cm), 4 in. (10 cm), 6 in. (15 cm), and 8 in. (20 cm) (Figure 3).

Figure 3

6. Put the funnel into the top of the bottle.
7. Set the bottle inside the sink under the faucet.
8. Plug the end of the straw with your finger.
9. Turn on the water at low pressure and fill the bottle to the top.
10. Without taking your finger off the straw, move the bottle outside to where the ground is level and can get wet without damaging nearby objects.
11. Place the ruler so that the zero end of it starts where the straw ends (Figure 4).

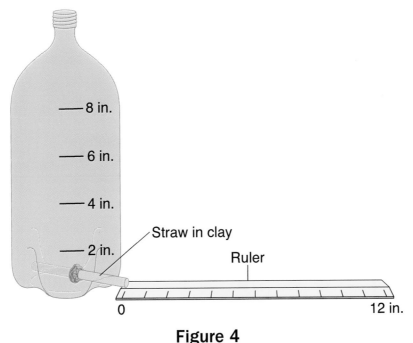

Figure 4

12. Remove your finger from the straw.

13. Watch the bottle carefully. When the water level drops to the 8-in. (20-cm) mark, see where the water flow is hitting the ruler.

14. Record the number.

15. Repeat steps 13 and 14 for each mark on the bottle.

16. Note that a dam holding back a large amount of water will have greater water pressure pushing on the bottom of the dam. Because of this, dams are typically wider on the bottom.

17. Using the knowledge gained from the first part of the experiment, build a model river and a dam.

18. Fill the storage container with sand.

19. Wet the sand in the middle.

20. With your hands, dig a deep riverbed in the sand running the length of the container (Figure 5).

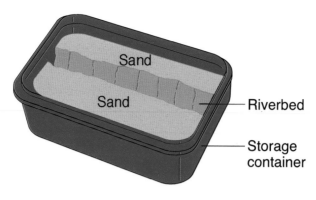

Figure 5

21. Using rocks and craft sticks, design and build a dam in the middle of the river bed that will allow only a small amount of water to pass through.

22. Pour water into the riverbed and observe how well your dam performs.

23. Evaluate the results and make adjustments to your design.

24. Repeat steps 21 to 23 and create a dam that does not allow any water to pass through.

 **Observations**

1. At which mark did the water shoot out the furthest?
2. What does this tell you about the water pressure?
3. Why are dams typically built wider at the bottom?
4. Were your dam designs in the second part of the experiment successful? Why or why not?

Our Findings

Please refer to the Our Findings appendix at the back of this volume.

Further Reading

"Dam." *The Columbia Encyclopedia*, 6th ed. 2008. Available online. URL: http://www.encyclopedia.com/doc/1E1-dam.html. Accessed January 3, 2010. Information about dams and examples of dams around the world.

"Hoover Dam." U.S. Bureau of Reclamation. 2009. Available online. URL: http://www.usbr.gov/lc/hooverdam/. Accessed January 3, 2010. Official Web site of the Hoover Dam, located at the Colorado River.

Sharpe, Elizabeth. *In the Shadow of the Dam: The Aftermath of the Mill River Flood of 1874.* New York: Free Press, 2007. A historical look at the disaster that occurred in 1874 when a dam failed, killing many people.

Stevens, Joseph. *Hoover Dam: An American Adventure.* Norman, OK: University of Oklahoma Press, 1990. History of and details about Hoover Dam. Includes photographs.

"Three Gorges Dam." *International Rivers.* 2009. Available online. URL: http://www.internationalrivers.org/china/three-gorges-dam. Accessed January 3, 2010. Information about the world's largest hydroelectric plant, located in China.

8. MODELING "ASPHALT"

Introduction

People drive their cars over it every day. You might walk on it, ride your bike over it, or even watch it being made. "It" is *asphalt*, a thick, black, sticky, tar-like substance used to hold together rocks in road *construction*. When asphalt is heated, it turns into a *viscous* liquid, but it hardens as it cools, eventually becoming a solid. Roads are typically made from a combination of rocks and asphalt, with asphalt serving as a *binder* for the *aggregates*. The exact amounts of asphalt and rock, as well as the type of rocks and size of rocks, used in road construction depend on the ground conditions and the *climate*. Natural asphalt was used in ancient times in the Middle East as *mortar* for building, to cement objects in place, and for waterproofing. Ancient Egyptians sometimes used natural asphalt for the *mummification* process. People in other parts of the world used asphalt, too, such as Native Americans who used *asphaltum*, a naturally occurring form, as an *adhesive*. The United States started using asphalt to *pave* roads as early as 1870. Today, most asphalt used in the United States is for asphalt *concrete* for road paving. Typically, the mixture contains only 5 percent asphalt and 95 percent aggregates, such as stone, gravel, or sand. Fortunately, asphalt can be *recycled*, so when roads are torn up, the asphalt can be reused to build new roads.

In this experiment, you will simulate road asphalt by creating chocolate "asphalt," a combination of thick, hot liquid with dry "aggregates."

 Time Needed
40 minutes

What You Need

- cocoa powder, 1/3 cup (77 grams [g])
- milk, 1/2 cup (118 ml)
- butter, 1 stick
- sugar, 2 cups (460 g)
- stove
- large metal pot or saucepan
- large stirring spoon
- large bowl
- rolling pin
- measuring cups
- wax paper, 2 sheets, each about 12 in. by 24 in. (30.5 cm by 61 cm)
- chopped walnuts, 1/2 cup (115 g)
- shredded coconut, 1/2 cup (77 g)
- quick-cooking oats, 1 cup (230 g)
- old-fashioned oats, 1 cup (230 g)

Safety Precautions

Please review and follow the safety guidelines at the beginning of this volume. Adult supervision is recommended when heating any substance. Students with food allergies or diabetes should not eat foods that pose a danger to their health.

What You Do

1. In the large pot, over medium heat, combine 1/3 cup cocoa powder, 1/2 cup milk, 1 stick of butter, and 2 cups of sugar until the mixture is a thick, smooth liquid (Figure 1). The resulting liquid is like asphalt at 300 degrees Fahrenheit (300°F).

Figure 1

2. Combine 1/2 cup walnuts, 1/2 cup shredded coconut, 1 cup quick-cooking oats, and 1 cup old-fashioned oats in a large bowl. In real asphalt, different types and sizes of rocks are used depending on the climate and area being paved.

3. Mix the dry ingredients.

4. Pour the chocolate asphalt into the bowl.

5. Stir until all the particles are coated with chocolate (Figure 2). The mixture becomes more difficult to stir as it cools because it hardens, just as asphalt does, when it cools.

Figure 2

6. Scoop the mixture out of the bowl and place the mixture on a sheet of wax paper (Figure 3).

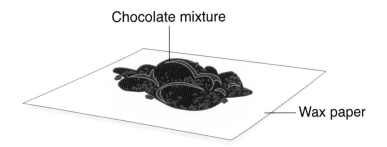

Figure 3

7. Place a top sheet of wax paper over the chocolate mixture (Figure 4).

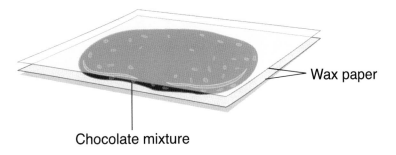

Figure 4

8. Use the rolling pin over the top sheet of wax paper to flatten the chocolate asphalt until it is no more than 1/3 in. thick. Real asphalt is spread by a heavy roller to ensure that the air is pushed out of its mixture, making the asphalt stronger.

9. Place your hand over the top sheet of wax paper and feel the heat. That is like actual asphalt, which is still hot just after being rolled.

10. Once the chocolate asphalt has cooled, peel off the wax paper.

11. Observe that the components used to create it are still visible.

12. Eat it and enjoy!

 **Observations**

1. How does this activity model paving asphalt?

2. What was the purpose of the melted chocolate mixture—e.g., why not just use the dry ingredients?

3. Under which field of engineering does road paving fall? What other everyday activities that we observe might be in this category?

Our Findings

Please refer to the Our Findings appendix at the back of this volume.

Further Reading

"Asphalt." *The Columbia Encyclopedia*, 6th ed. 2008. Available online. URL: http://www.encyclopedia.com/doc/1E1-asphalt.html. Accessed December 20, 2009. Short entry defining asphalt.

"Asphalt Concrete Mix Design and Field Control." U.S. Department of Transportation Federal Highway Administration, 1988. Available online. URL: http://www.fhwa.dot.gov/legsregs/directives/techadvs/ t504027.htm. Accessed December 20, 2009. Official Web site of the U.S. government detailing guidelines and questions for the mixing and use of asphalt concrete.

Capachi, Nick, and John Capachi. *Excavation and Grading Handbook*. Carlsbad, CA: Craftsman Book Company, 2005. Written by experienced contractors, includes information on laying and removing asphaltic concrete.

Knowledge Masters Plus: How Things Are Made. London: Chrysalis Children's Books: 2004. An illustrated children's book including information on how roads are made.

"Pavement." *The Columbia Encyclopedia*, 6th ed. 2008. Available online. URL: http://www.encyclopedia.com/doc/1E1-pavement.html. Accessed December 20, 2009. Explains the purpose of pavement and the materials used.

"What's New." U.S. Department of Transportation, Federal Highway Administration, 2009. Available online. URL: http://www.fhwa.dot. gov/new.html. Accessed December 20, 2009. Official Web site of the U.S. government detailing the latest road projects and information related to transportation.

9. CREATING A FULL-SIZE HOVERCRAFT

Introduction

Sir John Isaac Thorneycroft (1843–1928), a British ship builder, discovered that ships moved faster when their *hulls* were *lubricated* with air. Little did he know that this was the first step toward the development of *hovercraft*. Sir Christopher Sydney Cockerell (1910-99), a British engineer, took this concept further to invent the first true hovercraft. His goal was to build a craft that could both float on air and travel over water for practical purposes. The idea was that the air being generated would *propel* the vehicle, thus reducing the *friction* between the water and the craft. Believe it or not, he tested his theories with hair dryers and tin cans, items that you can find in your home. He experimented by placing the smaller can inside the larger one, then forcing air into the cans using a hair dryer. He discovered that the downward *force* of air was greater when there was one can inside another than when there was just one can alone.

Cockerell eventually built a full-size working model of his idea, obtained a *patent* for it, and launched his *prototype* in 1959. It was large enough to hold 4 people and could travel at speeds up to 28 miles per hour (45 km/hr). His craft worked so well that passengers were able to cross the English Channel on it.

Basically, a hovercraft is simply an air-cushion *vehicle*. The vehicle is able to ride over a smooth surface using high-pressure air that is pushed downward in a controlled manner. Today, these craft are used for both civilian and military purposes, carrying passengers or transporting large equipment. Each craft has a *skirt*, a curtain around the base. An engine forces high-pressure air under the vehicle and the air is then trapped under the skirt, forcing it to rise. This allows the hovercraft to travel over both land and water, which is why a hovercraft is considered an *amphibious* vehicle. Hovercraft can even travel over difficult *terrain*, such as swampland.

You can follow in the footsteps of a famous engineer and create your own full-size hovercraft, one that can actually carry people. In this experiment, you will build your own air-cushion vehicle. By completing this hands-on activity, you will learn firsthand how to engineer a vehicle that has a history of multiple applications, as well as create a fun ride (supervised) for you and your friends.

Time Needed

1 hour

What You Need

- plywood disk, 48 inches (in.) (122 centimeters [cm]) round and 3/8-in. (1 cm) or 1/2-in. (1.3 cm) thick
- plastic sheet, such as a plastic drop cloth from a paint store or an old plastic shower curtain, 1 ft (30.5 cm) larger than the plywood
- leaf blower or Shopvac™ with blower outlet, preferably battery powered
- small plastic disk, such as a coffee can lid, about 6 in. (15.2 cm) in diameter and 1/8 in. (0.3 cm) thick
- short wood screws, 5 or 6
- fender washers, 2
- smooth floor in a large empty area, such as a gym or basketball court
- electric saber drill
- razor
- staple gun with staples
- electric screwdriver
- duct tape
- measuring tape

pen or pencil

 an adult

 another partner

Safety Precautions

Caution: An adult *must* handle all power tools, such as electric saws, drills, leaf blowers, and other instruments such as staple guns. Have items cut to size at a local lumberyard rather than cutting them yourself. Always be careful when handling sharp objects, such as a razor, box cutter, knife, or sharp scissors. Please review and follow the safety guidelines at the beginning of this volume.

What You Do

1. Using the measuring tape and the pen, mark the exact center of the large plywood disk.

2. Using the same instruments, make a mark half way between the center and the edge of the disk (Figure 1).

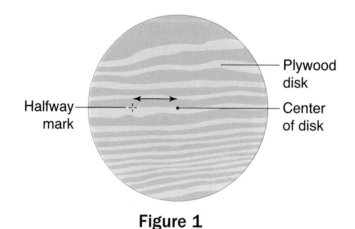

Figure 1

3. Place the mouth of the leaf blower on the mark and trace around it.

4. Have an adult cut out a hole in the plywood where you traced the mouth of the leaf blower. (They may use a drill or saw.)

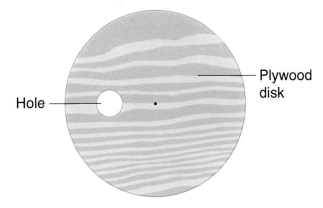

Hole

Plywood disk

Figure 2

5. Place the plywood disk on top of the plastic sheet.

6. Fold the plastic sheet up over the edge of the plywood all around and have an adult use the staple gun to staple the plastic into place tightly, but do not tear the plastic.

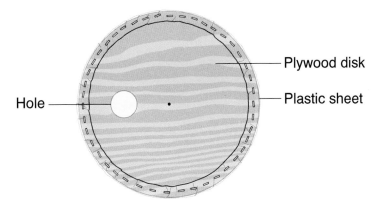

Hole

Plywood disk

Plastic sheet

Figure 3

7. Turn the plywood on its side. (You must have a partner to help you!)

8. Place the small plastic coffee can lid over the center of the plastic-covered side of the plywood.

9. Have an adult use the electric screwdriver to insert the screws through the uncovered side of the plywood through the coffee lid on the other side to secure it in place (Figure 4). The screws should go around the edges of the plastic lid.

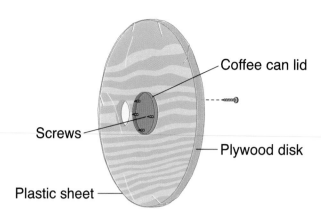

Figure 4

10. Put down the plywood with the plastic-covered side facing up.

11. About 2 to 3 in. from the edge of the plastic lid, have an adult use the razor to cut 6 vent holes in the plastic sheet around the lid. Each hole should be about 2 in. (5.1 cm) in diameter (Figure 5).

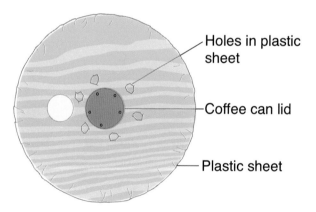

Figure 5

12. Place small strips of duct tape in between the holes to prevent tearing the plastic.

13. Turn the plywood over so the uncovered side is on top again and place it on the floor.

14. Place the leaf blower on top of the plywood and stick the mouth through the hole.

15. Use duct tape to secure the mouth of the leaf blower in place.

16. You have built a hovercraft! To prepare it for a ride, have some people hold it and lift it off the ground a few inches (about 7 cm).

17. Turn on the leaf blower and let the plastic fill with air.

18. Watch your hovercraft float!

 **Observations**

1. What is serving as the "engine" for your hovercraft?

2. What material comprises the skirt?

3. Explain how your hovercraft operates.

4. Why would a hair dryer not be appropriate for your hovercraft's engine?

5. If you were a hovercraft engineer, what changes to the design would you make and what purpose would these changes serve?

Our Findings

Please refer to the Our Findings appendix at the back of this volume.

Further Reading

Boileau, John. *Fastest in the World: The Saga of Canada's Revolutionary Hydrofoils*. Halifax, Canada: Formac, 2004. Recounts the history behind the fastest warship of the time, a hydrofoil based on a hovercraft prototype.

Chambers, John Whiteclay, II. "Helicopters." *The Oxford Companion to American Military History*. 2000. Accessed October 5, 2010. An article about helicopters, that includes those that can not only take off and land quickly but also hover in place.

Encyclopædia Britannica. 2009. "Cockerell, Sir Christopher Sydney." Available online. URL: http://www.britannica.com/EBchecked/ topic/123668/Sir-Christopher-Sydney-Cockerell. Accessed September 16, 2010. Contains a brief main entry regarding highlights of Sir Cockerell's life and related links regarding air-cushion machines.

"Helicopter." *The Columbia Encyclopedia*, 6th Edition. 2008. Accessed October 5, 2010. An article that explains how a helicopter is able to hover.

"Hydrofoil." *The Columbia Encyclopedia*, 6th Edition. 2008. Accessed October 5, 2010. Short article explaining the nature of the hydrofoil, a water craft that hovers above the surface of the water.

Jackson, Kevin. *Discover the Hovercraft*. Ashburn, VA: Flexitech LLC, 2004. Reviews the history of the hovercraft, as well as types and applications of engines found in the craft. Also includes alternative designs for building hovercraft.

Winklareth, Robert. *Naval Shipbuilders of the World: From the Age of Sail to the Present Day*. Barnsley, South Yorkshire, UK: Chatham Publishing, 2000. Details the advances made in shipbuilding over the years and the people who engineered the ships.

10. TESTING THE DURABILITY OF DIFFERENT BUILDING MATERIALS

Introduction

Structures can be built from different types of materials. The materials selected for a project will depend on the use of the structure, the height of the structure, local building codes, and *aesthetics*. Engineers must determine the best but most *cost-effective* materials to use for a project to ensure a safe structure within a given *budget*. For small projects or for aesthetic purposes, bricks and pavers are commonly used. A brick is made of *ceramic* material and is used in *masonry*. Bricks were made in ancient times from mud that was shaped and dried, often fired to increase strength and *durability*. Today, clay is most commonly used for making bricks, though other materials from which they are made include *shale*, *calcium silicate*, *concrete*, or stone. Depending on the source materials for the brick and how they are dried or fired, the strength and appearance of the brick is determined.

In this experiment, you will test the strength of several types of bricks and *pavers* and determine which is the strongest of the materials tested.

Time Needed

60 minutes

What You Need

- a second-story balcony from which to drop the bricks
- 15 clay bricks

- ✎ 15 cement pavers
- ✎ 15 fire bricks (heat-resistant)
- ✎ 15 cement bricks
- ✎ pen or pencil
- ✎ ruler
- ✎ weights (weight-labeled rocks that you weighed previously can be substituted)
- ✎ bucket
- ✎ rope, about 2 feet (ft) (about 60 centimeters [cm])
- ✎ 2 saw horses (2 benches or other raised, strong surfaces can be substituted)

Safety Precautions

Please review and follow the safety guidelines at the beginning of this volume. Do not drop anything from the balcony unless you are sure there is no one down below. It is recommended that you put up caution signs to keep others out of that area. Adult supervision is recommended.

What You Do

1. Drop 1 brick from the second story.
2. Count how many pieces into which the brick broke that are larger than 1 inch (in.) (about 2 cm).
3. Record your observation on the data table.
4. Repeat steps 1 to 3 four more times.
5. Repeat steps 1 to 4 with each of the other 3 types of bricks or cement pavers.
6. Place 1 brick over 2 saw horses (Figure 1).

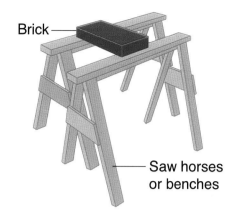

Figure 1

7. Hang the rope over the brick (Figure 2).

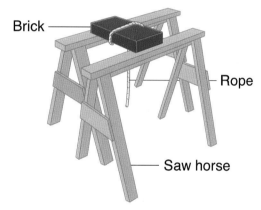

Figure 2

8. Tie the end of the rope to the bucket.

9. Keep adding weights to the bucket, keeping track of the total weight added, until the brick breaks. It is possible that, despite filling the bucket, one or more of the types of materials being tested might not break. If so, indicate on the data table that it did not break.

10. Record the amount of weight required for the brick to snap.

11. Empty the bucket.

12. Repeat steps 6 to 11 four more times.

13. Repeat steps 6 to 12 with the other bricks or pavers.

14. Calculate the averages for all your measurements on the data table.

Data Table		
Materials	Number of pieces after dropped from balcony	Weight required to break brick
Clay brick 1		
Clay brick 2		
Clay brick 3		
Clay brick 4		
Clay brick 5		
Average		
Cement paver 1		
Cement paver 2		
Cement paver 3		
Cement paver 4		
Cement paver 5		
Average		
Fire brick 1		
Fire brick 2		
Fire brick 3		
Fire brick 4		

(continued)

Fire brick 5		
Average		
Cement brick 1		
Cement brick 2		
Cement brick 3		
Cement brick 4		
Cement brick 5		
Average		

 Observations

1. The stronger the brick, the fewer pieces into which it will break when dropped. Which brick or paver seemed the strongest after this test? Which seemed the weakest?

2. A strong brick will be able to hold weight, especially important when constructing something large. Which brick or paver could hold the most weight before snapping? Which was least strong and broke with the least amount of weight added?

3. Based on your observations, which of the materials do you think would prove to be the strongest for building a structure?

4. Do bricks and pavers always have to be able to hold weight or withstand large forces? Explain and provide examples.

Our Findings

Please refer to the Our Findings appendix at the back of this volume.

Further Reading

"Brick." *The Columbia Encyclopedia*, 6th ed. 2008. Available online. URL: //www.encyclopedia.com/doc/1E1-brick.html. Accessed December 25, 2009. An article with a complete description of a common building material, along with its uses.

Campbell, James. *Brick: A World History*. London: Thames & Hudson, 2003. Beautiful photographs illustrate this book recounting the history of brick, its uses, famous structures made of brick, and modern-day bricks.

"Cement." *The Columbia Encyclopedia*, 6th ed. 2008. Available online. URL: //www.encyclopedia.com/doc/1E1-cement.html. Accessed December 25, 2009. Another article with a complete description of a material used in buildings, including how it was made.

Kreh, Dick. *Building With Masonry: Brick, Block, and Concrete*. Newtown, CT: Taunton Press, 1998. How-to book explaining materials needs, how to lay brick, and other related details.

"Mortar." *The Columbia Encyclopedia*, 6th ed. 2008. Available online. URL: //www.encyclopedia.com/doc/1E1-mortar1.html. Accessed December 25, 2009. A third article with a complete description of a common building material.

11. TESTING THE EFFECTIVENESS OF SOUND BARRIERS

Introduction

Sound is actually made of sound *waves*, which can travel through *solids*, *liquids*, and *gases*, but not through a *vacuum*. We perceive sound via our sense of hearing, which picks up the *vibrations* of the sound waves. The waves consist of *longitudinal*, or *compression*, waves, as well as *transverse* waves. Sound waves, like other waves, have *frequency*, *wavelength*, *period*, *amplitude*, speed, and direction. Sound is measured in units called *decibels* (dB). Measuring sound levels is especially important when trying to reduce noise.

The scientific study of the *absorption* and *reflection* of sound is called *acoustics*. *Acoustic engineering* is a special branch of engineering that focuses on the application of acoustics technology. Acoustics can be used to enhance sounds, such as in a concert hall, or to reduce sound levels to help diminish *noise pollution*. Everyday traffic on a busy highway contributes to overall noise pollution. In order to reduce such noise pollution, engineers have designed *barriers* to block some of the sound from reaching beyond the highway, hopefully reducing traffic noise levels for the local residents.

In this experiment, you will measure the noise levels near a highway and test the effectiveness of different types of sound barriers.

Time Needed

about 2 hours

What You Need

✎ 2 digital decibel meters with calibrators

- ✐ 1 hard hat
- ✐ 1 safety vest
- ✐ tape measure, 30 feet (ft) (about 10 meters [m])
- ✐ highway with steady traffic
- ✐ a partner
- ✐ paper, a few sheets
- ✐ 2 pens
- ✐ stopwatch or wristwatch

Safety Precautions

Please review and follow the safety guidelines at the beginning of this volume. Exercise caution when conducting experiments near traffic. Adult supervision is recommended, along with permission from your local police station.

What You Do

1. During the daytime, go to the highway and find an open area near the highway where there is no sound barrier and the area is safe.

2. Put on your safety gear of vest and hard hat. The hat will protect your head from any small rocks that might be kicked up into the air by traffic, and the vest will help motorists see you.

3. Set up 1 decibel meter about 15 ft (5 m) in from the highway.

4. Calibrate the meter according to the instructions and equipment that came with the meter.

5. Have your partner do steps 3 and 4 an additional 15 ft (5 m) from your location so that the second meter is 30 ft (10 m) from the highway.

6. Over a 10-minute period, both you and your partner should record the LEQ (average sound level) and the Max (highest sound level) readings from your decibel meters every 30 seconds for a total of 20 readings of LEQ and 20 readings of the Max.

7. Move your experiment further up or down the highway where there is a concrete barrier at the side of the highway.

8. Repeat steps 2 to 6.

9. Move your experiment to a part of the highway where large trees and bushes have been planted as a barrier.

10. Repeat steps 2 to 6.

11. Move your experiment to a part of the highway where an earth berm is used as a barrier.

12. Repeat steps 2 to 6.

 **Observations**

1. Was there a difference between decibel readings with and without a barrier present?

2. Which barrier provided the most reduction in noise?

3. Try testing the decibel meters farther away than 30 ft (10 m) from the barriers and the highway. Did this change your results? If so, how?

4. Why are sound barriers constructed near highways?

5. In your opinion, what other materials might create better sound barriers? On what is your opinion based?

Our Findings

Please refer to the Our Findings appendix at the back of this volume.

Further Reading

Acoustics.org. 2009. Available online. URL: http://www.acoustics. org/. Accessed December 23, 2009. Official Web site of the Acoustical Society of America, an association devoted to information about the field of acoustics.

Karpelenia, Jenny. *Sound*. Logan, UT: Perfection Learning, 2004. Children's book explaining how sound is generated, measured, and used.

Kosko, Bart. *Noise*. New York: Viking Adult, 2006. Book about noise pollution, causes of noise, and noise-canceling technology.

"Noise Pollution Clearinghouse." 2009. *Nonoise.org*. Available online. URL: http://www.nonoise.org/. Accessed December 23, 2009. Community organization dedicated to reducing noise pollution.

Russell, Dan. "Acoustics and Vibration Animations." 2001. Available online. URL: http://paws.kettering.edu/~drussell/demos.html. Accessed December 23, 2009. Provides succinct definitions related to acoustics, as well as animated figures.

12. MAKING A WINDMILL

Introduction

Windmills are machines that capture and convert the wind's energy to the energy of motion, specifically *rotational energy*. Windmills were used in the past to power *grinding mills*, *sawmills*, and *papermills*. Windmills actually date as far back as 9th-century Persia. There are several types of windmills, usually characterized by their *axis*. Some of these include *vertical-axis windmills*, *fixed horizontal-axis windmills*, and *horizontal-axis windmills* that move toward the wind. It is thought that several popular phrases arose from the use of windmills. When the winds died down, the windmills stopped and the grain was no longer being ground in the mill, leading to the expression to "grind to a halt." Some believe that when the grain was rubbed between the thumb and another finger to test for *coarseness*, another saying came into being: "rule of thumb."

Today, however, windmills are again being *manufactured* because they can capture a *renewable resource*: wind power. However, these windmills are designed differently from the windmills of the past and can often be found on "wind farms" where many windmills are positioned to *harness* the wind energy.

In this activity, you will create a model windmill and consider improvements in its design.

Time Needed

35 minutes

What You Need

✎   1 sheet of card stock, any color

- scissors
- small lump of modeling clay
- 1 large, disposable plastic cup
- pencil with an eraser, new, unsharpened
- pen
- ruler
- pushpin

Safety Precautions

Please review and follow the safety guidelines at the beginning of this volume.

What You Do

1. Trace the template (Figure 1) for the windmill sails on the card stock.

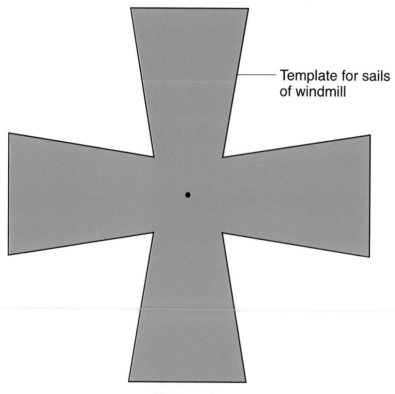

Template for sails of windmill

Figure 1

2. Cut out the template from the card stock for the windmill sails.

3. Poke a hole in the center of the bottom of the plastic cup with the pen (Figure 2).

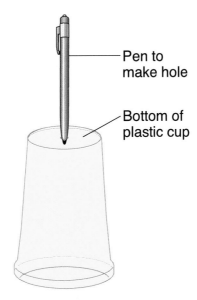

Pen to
make hole

Bottom of
plastic cup

Figure 2

4. Insert the pencil into the cup through the hole, with the eraser side outside the hole. Make sure the eraser end of the pencil is sticking up about 6 inches (in.) (15 centimeters [cm]) from the bottom of the cup (Figure 3).

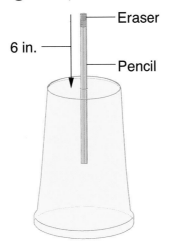

Eraser

6 in.

Pencil

Figure 3

5. Use the modeling clay on both the inside and outside of the cup to hold the pencil in place (Figure 4).

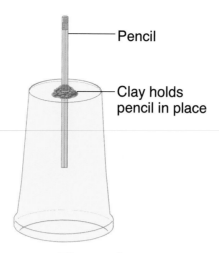

Figure 4

6. Stick the pushpin through the center of the card stock windmill sails and into the side of the eraser (Figure 5).

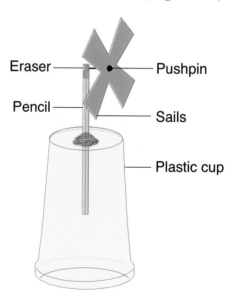

Figure 5

7. Bend each of the sails of the windmill slightly in the same direction (Figure 6).

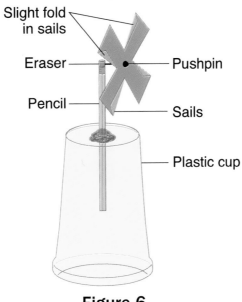

Slight fold
in sails

Eraser —

Pushpin

Pencil —

— Sails

— Plastic cup

Figure 6

8. Blow on the sails.

 **Observations**

1. How well did your windmill work?
2. What changes to the sails can you make to improve the design of the windmill and make the sails turn faster?
3. What are some of the uses of windmills?

Our Findings

Please refer to the Our Findings appendix at the back of this volume.

Further Reading

Baker, T. *American Windmills: An Album of Historic Photographs*. Norman, OK: University of Oklahoma Press, 2007. Contains about 200 photographs of windmills in the United States and shows their uses.

Gipe, Paul. *Wind Power, rev. ed*. White River Junction, VT: Chelsea Green Publishing Company, 2004. Explains the different types of wind technologies, as well their economic impact.

"Overview of Wind Energy in California." The California Energy Commission. 2009. Available online. URL: http://www.energy.ca.gov/wind/overview.html. Accessed December 22, 2009. Locates wind farms in California, provides photographs, and explains how wind power is harnessed and used.

"Renewable Wind." *Energy Kids*. U.S. Energy Information Administration. 2009. Available online. URL: http://tonto.eia.doe.gov/kids/energy.cfm?page=wind_home-basics. Accessed December 22, 2009. Information for children regarding how wind occurs on the Earth and how wind turbines work.

Tabak, John. *Wind and Water*. New York: Facts On File, 2009. Describes conventional wind power and some newer technologies that are being introduced to harnass the power of ocean currents, waves, and temperature.

"Windmill Tours: Palm Springs, California." *Windmilltours.com*. 2009. Available online. URL: http://www.windmilltours.com/. Accessed December 22, 2009. Information on scheduling a tour of the wind farm in Palm Springs, Calif.

13. MAKING A WATERWHEEL

Introduction

Waterwheels have been around for centuries. Evidence of the use of waterwheels has been linked to Mesopotamia, the Roman Empire, China, India, medieval Europe, and modern Europe. The most common use of the waterwheel was in *mills*, such as flour mills and paper mills for moving heavy stones for grinding. Waterwheels usually consist of a large metal or wooden wheel and numerous paddles, blades, or buckets to catch the flow of water, causing the wheel to move. Waterwheels are classified according to how the water hits the device relative to the *axle*. Some types of waterwheels include horizontal wheel, undershot wheel, breastshot wheel, overshot wheel, and backshot wheel.

In this experiment, you will make a waterwheel and test it for its ability to move a *load* using the power of water.

Time Needed

1 to 2 hours

What You Need

- corrugated cardboard or foam board, at least 2 feet (ft) by 2 ft (60 centimeters [cm] by 60 cm)
- pushpins, 24
- pen or pencil
- wooden skewer

- compass for making circles
- protractor
- scissors
- ruler
- sink with running water
- string, about 1 ft (about 30 cm)
- empty foam egg carton
- 3 or 4 pennies

Safety Precautions

Please review and follow the safety guidelines at the beginning of this volume.

What You Do

1. Cut out ten 1.5-in. by 2-in. (about 4-cm by 5-cm) segments of cardboard.
2. Using your compass, trace 2 circles on the cardboard, each with a 6-in. (15-cm) diameter.
3. Cut out the 2 circles.
4. Poke holes through the center of both circles.
5. Trace the pattern for the stands onto the cardboard (Figure 1) and cut out two of them.

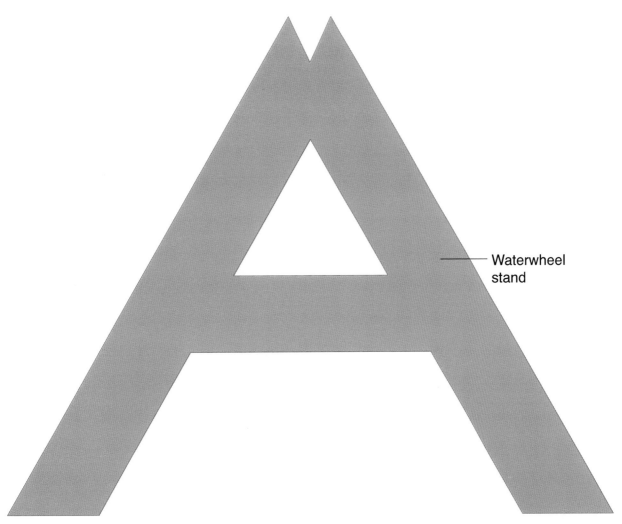

Waterwheel
stand

Figure 1

6. Trace the pattern for the support beams onto the cardboard
   (Figure 2) and cut out two of them.

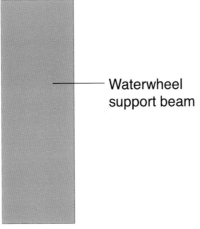

Waterwheel
support beam

Figure 2

7. Using the protractor, mark off intervals of 40 degrees (40°) on one of the circles (Figure 3).

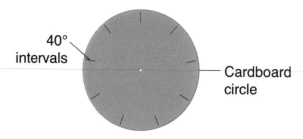

Figure 3

8. Using the pushpins, attach to the circle the 10 short pieces of cardboard you cut out and attach them along the intervals you just marked (Figure 4).

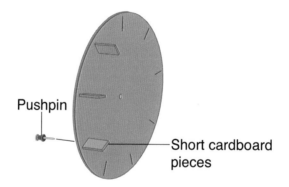

Figure 4

9. Attach the second circle to the other side of the 10 pieces (Figure 5).

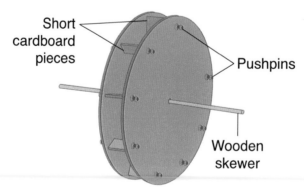

Figure 5

10. Slip the wooden skewer through the center of both circles (Figure 5).

11. Using pushpins, attach the support beams to the stands so that the assembly can stand up on its own (Figure 6).

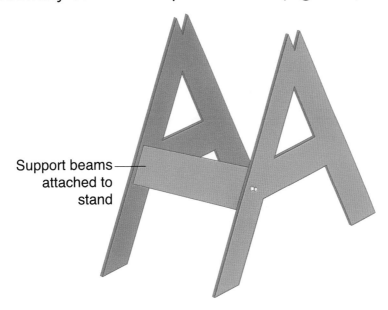

Support beams attached to stand

Figure 6

12. Rest the skewer on top of the stands (Figure 7).

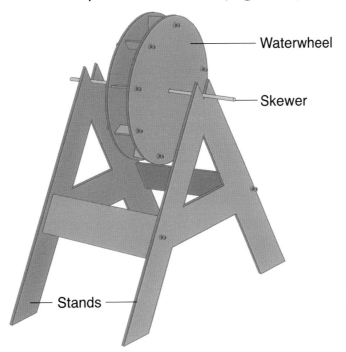

Waterwheel

Skewer

Stands

Figure 7

13. Put the waterwheel in a sink.

14. Turn on the faucet slowly so that the water comes out under low pressure and hits the paddles of your waterwheel (Figure 8).

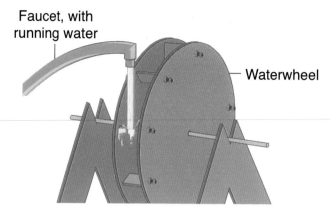

Figure 8

15. Observe the way the wheel moves under the stream of water.

16. Turn off the faucet.

17. Cut out 1 egg holder from the egg carton (Figure 9) to make a "foam bucket."

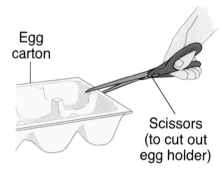

Figure 9

18. Poke holes in the sides of the piece you cut out.

19. Cut off a few inches of string and tie each end to the holes of the little foam bucket you have created, forming a handle (Figure 10).

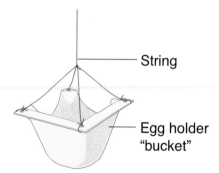

Figure 10

20. Tie the rest of the string to the handle you just made.

21. Cut the string so that, when you tie the other end of the string to the skewer of the waterwheel, the "bucket" is just barely touching the sink (Figure 11).

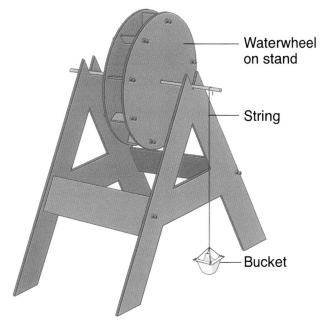

Waterwheel on stand

String

Bucket

Figure 11

22. Put a few pennies in the bucket.

23. Repeat steps 14 to 16 and observe what happens to the bucket.

 **Observations**

1. What happened to your waterwheel when you turned on the water?

2. What happened to the bucket when it was attached to the waterwheel and you turned on the water?

3. Test the capacity of your waterwheel to move more weight by adding more pennies to the bucket and turning on the water. What is the maximum number of pennies the waterwheel can lift?

4. How do you think waterwheels were used in mills?

Our Findings

Please refer to the Our Findings appendix at the back of this volume.

Further Reading

Gies, Joseph, and Frances Gies. *Cathedral, Forge, and Water Wheel: Technology and Invention in the Middle Ages*. New York: Harper Perennial, 1995. A look at the technology of the Middle Ages.

"Hydraulic Machine." *The Columbia Encyclopedia*, 6th ed. 2008. Available online. URL: //www.encyclopedia.com/doc/1E1-hydraul-m. html. Accessed January 2, 2010. Explanation of devices powered by motion or pressure of liquid.

Reynolds, Terry. *Stronger Than a Hundred Men: The History of the Vertical Water Wheel*. Baltimore: Johns Hopkins University Press, 2002. A comprehensive history of the waterwheel and its uses.

Tabak, John. *Wind and Water*. New York: Facts On File, 2009. Describes conventional wind power and some newer technologies that are being introduced to harnass the power of ocean currents, waves, and temperature.

"Turbine." *The Columbia Encyclopedia*, 6th ed. 2008. Available online. URL: //www.encyclopedia.com/doc/1E1-turbine.html. Accessed January 2, 2010. Explanation of the hydraulic turbine, which replaced waterwheels.

"Water Wheel." *The Columbia Encyclopedia*, 6th ed. 2008. Available online. URL: //www.encyclopedia.com/doc/1E1-waterwhe.html. Accessed January 2, 2010. Short entry about the history and uses of the waterwheel.

14. DESIGNING A RUBE GOLDBERG MACHINE

Introduction

Rube Goldberg (1883–1970) was an American *cartoonist* who held a degree in *engineering*. He is best remembered for his inventions of complicated, comical *contraptions* that used a series of numerous *simple machines* to accomplish one small task. Today, any such machine is known as a Rube Goldberg device. Such contraptions typically have *gears*, paddles, alarms, and oftentimes even live animals to start the motion of the machine. Purdue University, located in Indiana, hosts an annual Rube Goldberg contest to see who can engineer the most complex contraption. To this day, Rube Goldberg's legacy lives on in cartoons, such as "Looney Tunes,"® depicting complicated devices to perform simple tasks and even in the concept behind the popular children's board game "Mouse Trap.®"

In this activity, you will design one or more Rube Goldberg machines based on materials you have available. You will then construct one or more of them and test your design to see if the final operation is accomplished.

Time Needed

3 to 4 hours

What You Need

- ✎ several sheets of plain white paper
- ✎ pencil

(Author's note: The following materials are suggested and can be modified based on what you have available.)

- duct tape
- plastic cups
- scissors
- marbles or small rubber balls
- pulleys
- string or rope
- dominoes
- cardboard tubes from inside paper towel rolls
- shoes or boots
- building blocks or Legos®
- pennies
- clay
- toy cars or trucks
- computer with Internet access

Safety Precautions

Please review and follow the safety guidelines at the beginning of this volume. Always follow Internet safety guidelines.

What You Do

1. Review examples of Rube Goldberg machines by visiting several Web sites including the following:

   http://www.rubegoldberg.com/

   http://www.purdue.edu/UNS/rube/rube.index.html

   http://mousetrapcontraptions.com/tips-9.html

2. Decide on a simple task that you want your machine to accomplish as an end result (e.g., to turn on an electronic device or to feed the cat; Figure 1).

Figure 1

3. Keeping in mind the materials you have available, sketch a diagram of the different machines needed to form the Rube Goldberg device and how each one is connected to the next. Remember: Once the machine is in motion, you should not have to be involved in keeping it running (Figure 2).

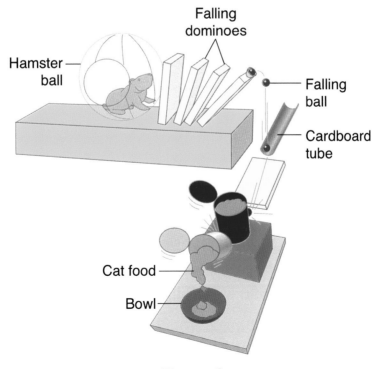

Figure 2

4. Select your best design and build a prototype of your device.

5. Test your device.

6. Evaluate the results and make any changes needed if the machine did not accomplish its task.

 **Observations**

1. Was your device the simplest way to complete the final task? Why or why not?

2. Did your prototype work? What changes, if any, did you need to make?

3. What materials would you need to create a more complex machine?

4. Would you consider entering a Rube Goldberg contest? If so, what task would your device accomplish? Research how to apply for the contest.

Our Findings

Please refer to the Our Findings appendix at the back of this volume.

Further Reading

Davis, Martin. *Rube Goldberg on Golf*. Alexandria, VA: American Geological Institute, 2009. Colorized version of Rube Goldberg's funny drawings about golf.

Goldberg, Rube. *Foolish Questions*. Landisville, PA: Coachwhip Publications, 2009. A reprint of Rube Goldberg's famous comic strip where foolish questions deserve foolish answers.

"Rube Goldberg." *RubeGoldberg.com*. 2009. Available online. URL: http://www.rubegoldberg.com/. Accessed January 1, 2010. Official Web site about Rube Goldberg, his life, and information about constructing his devices.

————. *The Columbia Encyclopedia*, 6th ed. 2008. Available online. URL: //www.encyclopedia.com/doc/1E1-GoldbergR.html. Accessed January 1, 2010. Short encyclopedia entry about Rube Goldberg and his legacy.

"Rube Goldberg Contest at Purdue." *Purdue.edu*. 2009. Available online. URL: http://www.purdue.edu/UNS/rube/rube.index.html. Accessed January 1, 2010. Official Web site of the annual contest at Purdue University for constructing Rube Goldberg machines.

Wolfe, Maynard Frank. *Rube Goldberg: Inventions!* New York: Simon & Schuster, 2000. A collection of Rube Goldberg's cartoons and invention designs.

15. BUILDING A MODEL SKYSCRAPER

Introduction

Skyscrapers are tall buildings that extend beyond the main skyline. Cities may have their own height requirements for a building to be classified a skyscraper, but there are several well-known buildings that are famous for their exceptional height. The Empire State Building in New York City is one such example, as is the Willis Tower (formerly known as the Sears Tower) in Chicago. For many years, the world's tallest building was located in Taiwan, called Taipei 101; it was *surpassed* by a new structure built in Dubai.

The term *skyscraper* became popular in the late 19th century when engineering designs allowed buildings to be built taller than before. Today, structures can be made even taller with the help of reinforced steel. The height and design of such structures is greatly influenced by the conditions being taken into account, including wind, weight, and *earthquakes*.

In this experiment, you will create a model skyscraper and perform weight and wind tests on it.

Time Needed

1 hour

What You Need

- 10 straws
- deck of playing cards

- ruler
- scissors
- 10 Gummi™ bears
- roll of transparent tape
- paper, a few sheets, unlined
- pencil
- hair blow-dryer
- electrical outlet, close at hand
- stopwatch or clock

Safety Precautions

Please review and follow the safety guidelines at the beginning of this volume. Adult supervision is recommended when working with electrical outlets.

What You Do

1. Study the materials you have available for building your skyscraper: straws, playing cards, tape, ruler, and scissors.

2. You have 1 hour to design and build a "skyscraper" model that is at least 14 inches (in.) (about 35 centimeters [cm]) high and can hold 10 Gummi™ bears on top without collapsing, as well as withstand the "wind" force from a hair blow-dryer.

3. Sketch some ideas for how you will design your skyscraper. Plan where supports might be placed to prevent collapse.

4. Select the most promising design and create your structure (Figure 1).

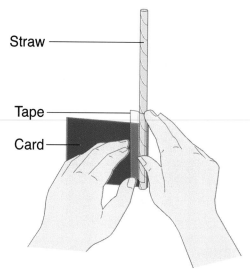

Figure 1

5. After 1 hour, measure your structure to ensure that it is at least 14 in. high.

6. Place the 10 Gummi™ bears on top of the structure (Figure 2).

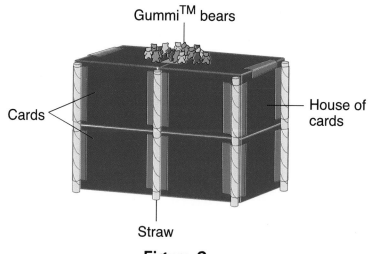

Figure 2

7. Record your observations.

8. Plug in the blow-dryer and hold it 14 in. away from your structure (Figure 3).

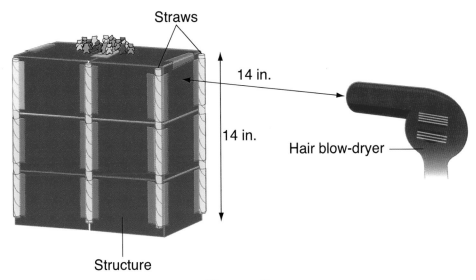

Figure 3

9. Turn it on low for 60 seconds.

10. Record your observations.

 **Observations**

1. Was your structure successful at holding the weight of the Gummi™ bears? Why or why not?

2. Was your structure successful at withstanding the wind? Why or why not?

3. What changes would you make to your design if you were going to make a taller structure?

4. What changes would you make to your design it you wanted it to withstand the blow-dryer on its highest setting?

Our Findings

Please refer to the Our Findings appendix at the back of this volume.

Further Reading

"Empire State Building." *The Empire State Building Official Internet Site*. Available online. URL: http://www.esbnyc.com/index2.cfm?CFID =36404004&CFTOKEN=40675109. Accessed December 21, 2009. The official Web site of New York City's Empire State Building, one of the world's tallest structures.

Pridmore, Jay. *Sears Tower: A Building Book from the Chicago Architectural Foundation*. Carpinteria, CA: Pomegranate, 2002. The story of one of the tallest buildings ever created, built expressly for one of the nation's largest retailers.

Skyscraperpage.com. Available online. URL: //skyscraperpage.com/. Accessed December 21, 2009. Web site for skyscraper enthusiasts including photographs, diagrams, and information.

"Taipei 101 Observatory." *Taipei-101.com*. Available online. URL: http://www.taipei-101.com.tw/en/DB/index.asp. Accessed December 21, 2009. Official Web site of the Taipei building observatory, includes links to other information about the building.

Tauranac, John. *Empire State Building: The Making of a Landmark*. New York: St. Martin's Griffin, 1997. Provides a history of the Empire State Building in New York City from the time that it was first conceptualized.

16. CONSTRUCTING A SKATEBOARD RAMP

Introduction

Skateboarding is the sport of riding and performing tricky, and often dangerous, *maneuvers* on a skateboard. Skateboarding is a fairly modern sport, and those who do it are referred to as "skaters." Originally, skateboarding tricks consisted of lifting some of the wheels off the ground and performing "wheelies." However, as the sport became more popular, skaters began building *engineering* ramps on which they could perform more complicated tricks. A *halfpipe* is a structure used in many extreme sports, including skateboarding, that is made of two *concave* ramps (or *quarterpipes*) facing each other. Prior to the advent of skate parks, early skaters were known for skating in empty swimming pools to achieve the same effect as the halfpipes. Some well-known skaters include Californians Tony Alva (1957–), considered one of the pioneers of skating and one of the first to make the sport popular, and Tony Hawk (1968–), known for his numerous wins in skateboarding competitions. However, both of these famous skaters have something in common: They practiced on ramps.

In this activity, you will follow a design to build a mini-skateboard ramp.

Time Needed

4 to 6 hours

What You Need

- 8 pieces of 2 by 4s, 4 feet (ft) (1.2 meters [m]) long

2 pieces of 3/4-inch (-in.) plywood, 4 ft by 8 ft (2.4 m)

 2 pieces of 3/8-in. plywood, 8 ft by 4 ft

 hammer

 measuring tape

 pencil

 jigsaw

 nails, about 60

Safety Precautions

Please review and follow the safety guidelines at the beginning of this volume. Adult supervision is required for this activity. Exercise caution when operating any type of machinery. Adult supervision is recommended for testing and using the ramp.

What You Do

1. Cut the 3/4-in. plywood in half lengthwise.
2. On 1 piece, draw a line starting 1.5 in. (3.8 centimeters [cm]) from the bottom, angling toward the top, ending about 8 in. (20.3 cm) from the opposite side (Figure 1).

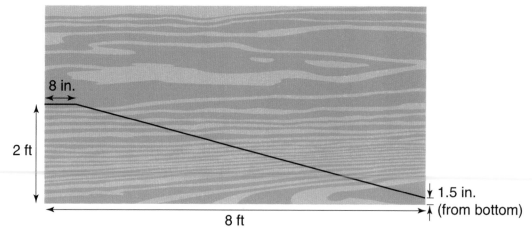

Figure 1

3. Cut out the shape.

4. Trace the shape onto the other half.

5. Cut out that shape.

6. Make a mark with a pencil every 8 in. along the angled edge of both pieces (Figure 2).

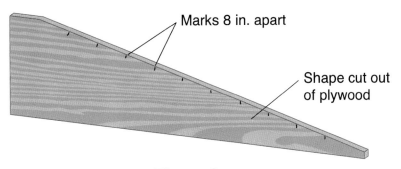

Marks 8 in. apart

Shape cut out of plywood

Figure 2

7. Nail in one 2 by 4 horizontally across the bottom between the cut out pieces using 2 nails on each side (Figure 3).

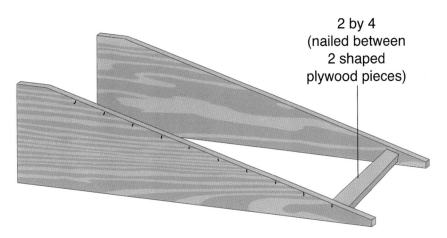

2 by 4 (nailed between 2 shaped plywood pieces)

Figure 3

8. About every 8 in., using 2 nails on each side, nail in 5 more 2 by 4s, and place them perpendicular rather than horizontal (Figure 4).

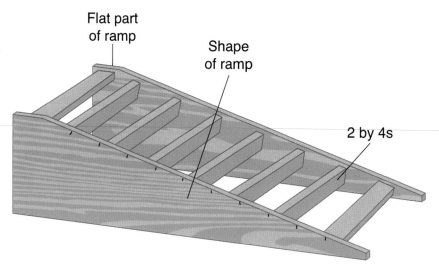

Figure 4

9. Nail in one more 2 by 4 at the beginning of the flat part of the ramp on top using 2 nails on each side (Figure 4).

10. Nail in one more 2 by 4 at the back of the top part of the ramp using 2 nails on each side (Figure 4).

11. Place the 3/8-in. plywood over the ramp.

12. With a pencil, trace where the plywood needs to be cut so that the entire ramp is covered in plywood. You will need to cut a second, smaller piece to cover the top part where the ramp is flat, and a third strip, even smaller, to create a transition from the ground to the ramp (Figure 5).

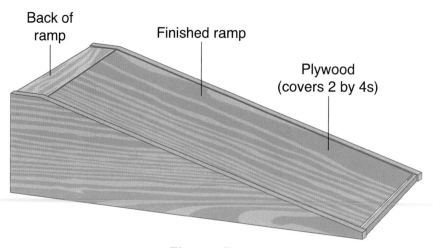

Figure 5

13. Nail the plywood in place onto the 2 by 4s.

 **Observations**

1. How can a ramp be used to accelerate and decelerate a skater?

2. What changes to the design would you make to increase the acceleration?

3. What happens if you put 2 curved ramps facing each other and skate down one of the ramps?

4. If you have the materials available, build a second identical ramp. Design a wooden box of the same height as your ramps and cover it with plywood. Place the box between the 2 ramps: You have built a "funbox." How well did your design work?

Our Findings

Please refer to the Our Findings appendix at the back of this volume.

Further Reading

"Action Sports." *ESPN.com*. 2009. Available online. URL: http://espn.go.com/action. Accessed January 3, 2010. Coverage of the "X Games," sports competitions based on skateboarding and other extreme non-traditional sports.

Friedman, Glenn. *Dogtown: The Legend of the Z Boys*. New York: Burning Flags Press, 2002. History, accompanied by photographs, of some of the original skateboarders in the 1970s.

Gifford, Clive. *Skateboarding*. New York: DK Children, 2006. Children's book about skateboarding, how to skateboard, and skateboarding tricks.

"Hawk, Tony." UXL Newsmakers. 2005. Available online. URL: http://www.encyclopedia.com/doc/1G2-3441500052.html. Accessed October 8, 2010. Background on skateboarder Tony Hawk and skateboarding in general.

"Machines, Simple." UXL Encyclopedia of Science. 2002. Available online. URL: http://www.encyclopedia.com/doc/1G2-3438100400.html. Accessed October 8, 2010. Encyclopedia article about simple machines that explains the inclined plane, the basis of a ramp.

"Skateboarding." *Skateboard.com*. 2009. Available online. URL: http://www.skateboard.com/. Accessed January 3, 2010. Web site with videos and news about skateboarding and skating events.

Skateboardpark.com. "Skateparks." Available online. URL: http://skateboardpark.com/. Accessed October 8, 2010. This article lists skateboard parks around the United States.

"Tony Hawk." *Tonyhawk.com*. 2009. Available online. URL: http://www.tonyhawk.com/. Accessed January 3, 2010. Official Web site of famous skateboarder Tony Hawk.

17. BUILDING AN IGLOO

Introduction

Igloos, or snow houses, are built by the *Inuits* (the Eskimo people of North America and Greenland). The name comes from *Iglu*, which is the Inuit word for house. Igloos are generally used as temporary *shelters* created from blocks of snow. There are three traditional types of igloos. The most common is a small igloo used as a temporary shelter. There is also a medium-sized igloo used semi-permanently as a *dwelling*. Finally, there is a large igloo that consists of two buildings, one temporary for special occasions and the other more permanent. These larger igloos can hold as many as 20 people.

When constructing an igloo, the hole remaining in the snow where the snow was removed for making blocks is used to create the bottom part of the igloo. It is common to have a tunnel leading to the entrance to prevent wind from entering the igloo and heat from escaping. In a traditional Inuit igloo, a stone lamp is used for heat, which causes slight melting of the ice blocks. However, the blocks refreeze, which actually strengthens the structure. The design of an igloo is simple, yet it is a *feat of engineering*.

In this activity, you will create a model igloo and analyze the application of the engineering *technology* used in its design.

Time Needed

2 hours

What You Need

✐   4 cups (1 liter) flour

- 1 1/2 cups (400 milliliters [ml]) water
- 1 cup (300 ml) salt
- 1 paper plate
- knife
- pencil
- 1 can of white frosting
- large bowl
- large stirring spoon
- rolling pin
- flat area or covered table to roll out dough
- ruler

Safety Precautions

Please review and follow the safety guidelines at the beginning of this volume. Adult supervision is recommended when handling such sharp objects as knives.

What You Do

1. Mix the flour, water, and salt in a large bowl. When you can no longer stir it with a spoon, use your hands.
2. Knead the dough for about 5 minutes.
3. Find a flat, clean surface where you can roll the dough.
4. Place the dough on the surface and use the rolling pin to roll it until it is about 1/3- to 1/2-in. thick (about 10 mm).
5. Using the ruler and the knife, cut out 50 "blocks" from the dough, each about 1/2 in. by 1/4 in. (about 10 mm by 5 mm). (Figure 1).

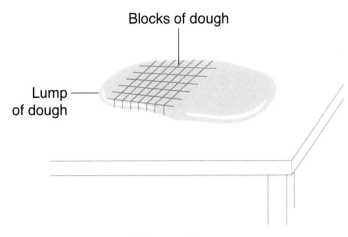

Figure 1

6. Place 4 blocks end to end (Figure 2).

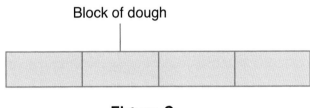

Figure 2

7. Cut the 4 blocks diagonally, as shown in Figure 3

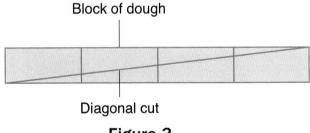

Figure 3

8. Discard the top portion of those cut blocks. The other blocks start the bottom of the igloo.

9. Turn the paper plate upside down.

10. Stand the cut blocks upright and place them along the rim of upside-down plate, using white frosting to hold them in place (Figure 4).

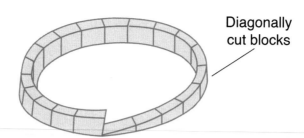

Figure 4

11. Continue adding blocks in a circle and pasting them in place with frosting (Figure 5).

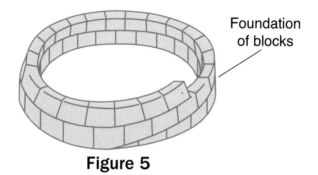

Figure 5

12. When you reach the first blocks you placed on the plate, continue adding blocks on top of them but tilt each layer slightly inward (Figure 6).

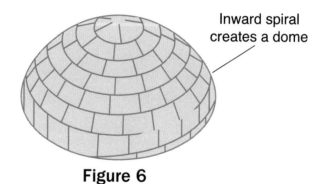

Figure 6

13. Continue spiraling inward until you create a dome (Figure 6).

14. Cut one last block to fit into the hole that is left on top (Figure 6).

15. Using the knife, cut out a doorway about 2 blocks high and use any leftover blocks to build a doorway, as in Figure 7.

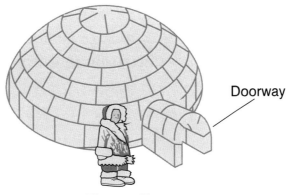

Figure 7

 **Observations**

1. How is the knowledge of the engineering of structures and domes helpful to building an igloo?
2. Why is an igloo only a temporary structure?
3. What other materials could you use for a model igloo?
4. How do you think this engineering technology could be applied to other structures?

Our Findings

Please refer to the Our Findings appendix at the back of this volume.

Further Reading

Gardiner, Lisa. "Inuit Culture, Traditions, and History." Regents of the University of Michigan, 2007. Available online. URL: //www.windows. ucar.edu/tour/link=/earth/polar/inuit_culture.html. Accessed December 20, 2009. Background information on the culture, clothing, and buildings of the Inuit people.

Giese, Paula. "Igloo-The Traditional Arctic Snow Dome." 1996. Available online. URL: //www.kstrom.net/isk/maps/houses/igloo. html. Accessed December 20, 2009. Provides a brief overview of the history of the igloo.

"Igloo." *The Columbia Encyclopedia*, 6th ed. 2008. Available online. URL: //www.encyclopedia.com/doc/1E1-igloo.html. Accessed December 20, 2009. Short encyclopedia entry on the purpose of an igloo.

Santella, Andrew. *The Inuit*. Chicago: Children's Press, 2000. Children's book about the Native Americans who lived in the far north of the country.

Yue, Charlotte. *The Igloo*. West Perth, Ont., Canada: Sandpiper, 1992. Illustrated children's book about the history of the Eskimos and their life inside igloos.

18. MAKING A DOOR ALARM

Introduction

One branch of engineering is *electrical engineering*, a field that relates to the application of *electricity* and *electromagnetism*. William Gilbert (1540–1603) was an English *physician* who later became what is believed to be one of the first electrical engineers. However, in the 19th century, other scientists became better known for their work with electricity, such as the German *physicist* George Ohm (1787–1854) and the English chemist and physicist Michael Faraday (1791–1867). In modern times, inventions *attributed* to this field of study include the radio, microwave ovens, *radar*, and computers. To become an electrical engineer, most people in the field earn a 4-year bachelor of science degree in electrical engineering and sometimes a postgraduate degree in the field. We all depend on the *technology* created and modified by electrical engineers for the many useful *devices* we have come to rely on every day.

In this experiment, you will create an electrical device, namely, an alarm for a door that will sound when the door is opened.

Time Needed

45 minutes

What You Need

- ✏ 1 wooden clothespin
- ✏ electrical tape, small roll
- ✏ scissors

- 3 stripped electrical wires, each about 5 inches (in.) (13 centimeters [cm])
- buzzer
- 9-volt battery
- wooden board, about 8 in. by 8 in. (20 cm)
- cardboard, 1 in. by 2 in. (2.5 cm by 5 cm)
- glue
- heavy object to weigh down the wood
- a door with a doorknob
- string, about 2 to 3 feet (ft) (2/3 meters [m] to 1 m)

Safety Precautions

Please review and follow the safety guidelines at the beginning of this volume. Exercise caution when dealing with batteries and electricity. Adult supervision is recommended.

What You Do

1. Tape the battery to the wooden board (Figure 1).

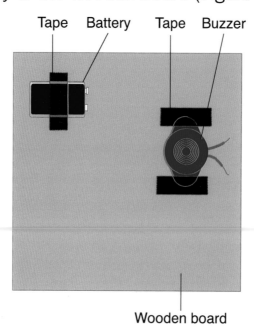

Tape   Battery   Tape   Buzzer

Wooden board

Figure 1

2. Tape the buzzer to the wooden board (Figure 1).

3. Wrap the grip end of each side of the open clothespin with a wire about 3 times, leaving the rest of the wire dangling (Figure 2). When the clothespin is closed, the wrapped part of the wires on each side should touch (Figure 3).

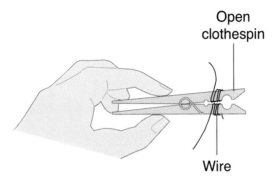

Open
clothespin

Wire

Figure 2

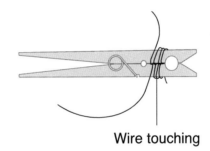

Wire touching

Figure 3

4. Attach one of the wires from the clothespin to the negative end of the battery (Figure 4). Secure the battery with electrical tape.

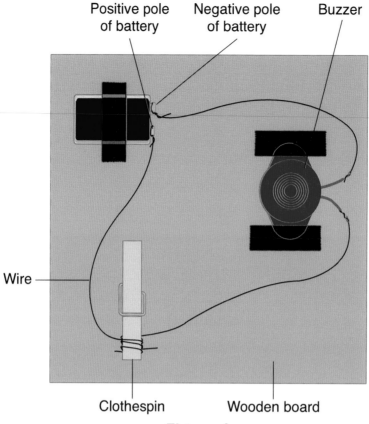

Positive pole of battery   Negative pole of battery   Buzzer

Wire

Clothespin   Wooden board

Figure 4

5. Connect the other wire from the clothespin to the buzzer (Figure 4).

6. Place a small piece of cardboard inside the clothespin to keep it from closing and to keep the wrapped part of the wires from touching (Figure 5).

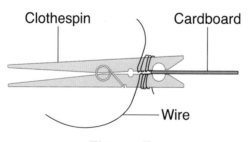

Clothespin   Cardboard

Wire

Figure 5

7. Connect the remaining wire from the positive end of the battery to the buzzer (Figure 4). Secure the wire with electrical tape.

8. Take out the cardboard from the clothespin and make sure that the buzzer sounds. If it does not, recheck all your connections.

9. Reinsert the cardboard inside the clothespin.

10. Glue the clothespin to the wooden board (Figure 4).

11. Attach one end of the string to the small piece of cardboard.

12. Tie the other end of the string around your doorknob (Figure 6).

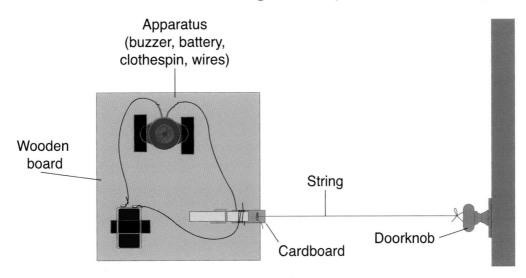

Apparatus
(buzzer, battery,
clothespin, wires)

Wooden
board

String

Doorknob

Cardboard

Figure 6

13. Place the wooden board with the attached buzzer so that when the string is pulled taut, the action of opening the door will pull it even tighter, resulting in the cardboard being pulled out of the clothespin and the buzzer sounding.

14. Weigh down the wood so that it cannot be easily moved.

 **Observations**

1. Why does the removal of the cardboard cause the buzzer to sound?

2. What else could you use for your alarm beside a buzzer to make a sound?

3. How else could you design a door alarm, now that you understand the principle behind it?

4. How is this technology helpful?

Our Findings

Please refer to the Our Findings appendix at the back of this volume.

Further Reading

Ashby, Darren. *Electrical Engineering 101: Everything You Should Have Learned in School . . . But Probably Didn't*, 2nd ed. Burlington, MA: Newnes, 2008. A practical guide for electrical engineers.

"Electromagnet." *The Columbia Encyclopedia*, 6th ed. 2008. http://www.encyclopedia.com/doc/1E1-electromg.html. Accessed December 26, 2009. Encyclopedia entry about electromagnets and how they work.

Kybett, Harry, and Earl Boysen. *All New Electronics Self-Teaching Guide*. Hoboken, NJ: Wiley, 2008. Book for electronics enthusiasts who want to do electrical projects on their own.

Mims, Forrest. *Getting Started in Electronics*. Lincolnwood, IL: Master Publishing, 2003. The equivalent of taking a crash course in electronics, teaches you how to make various electronic devices.

"Welcome to CalTech Electrical Engineering." *CalTech*. 2009. Available online. URL: http://www.ee2.caltech.edu/. Accessed December 26, 2009. The Web site of the electrical engineering department of Cal Tech University.

19. INVESTIGATING AND MAKING A MODEL OF THE SPACE SHUTTLE

Introduction

The *space shuttle* is a specially *engineered* aircraft designed to be able to travel to outer space and return to be reused. The space shuttle program began its first flights in 1982. The design of the space shuttle includes the *orbital vehicle*, which contains the *payload* and the crew, as well as the *booster rockets* and *external* tanks, which are required to launch the space shuttle. Once orbit is achieved, the external tanks are *jettisoned*. Because of the shuttle's large *cargo bay* and doors that can open out to unload the payload, the shuttle is considered unique. It is also the first spacecraft designed to be reused. Shuttle launches are run by NASA (National Aeronautics and Space Administration). The official NASA Web site has an extensive section devoted to the shuttle launches and can be accessed at www.nasa.gov.

In this activity, you will create a model of the space shuttle and learn about the shuttle's history and missions.

Time Needed

2 hours

What You Need

- ✎ 3 cardboard tubes from inside paper towel rolls
- ✎ empty oatmeal container, smaller size
- ✎ 2 small paper cups
- ✎ pencil

- measuring tape
- masking tape
- scissors
- glue, especially sticky
- construction paper, light gray and dark gray, at least 2 sheets of each color
- 4 dry beans
- dark-gray tempera paint
- small paintbrush
- paper towels, a few sheets
- computer with Internet access

Safety Precautions

Please review and follow the safety guidelines at the beginning of this volume. Always follow Internet safety guidelines when accessing the Internet.

What You Do

1. Cut off the top portion of both paper cups (Figure 1).

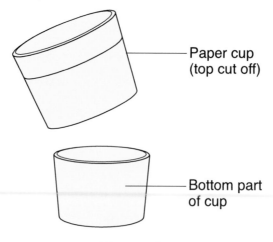

Figure 1

2. Place the bottom part of the cups upside down on a paper towel, and with the paint brush paint the outsides of the cups with dark-gray paint (Figure 2).

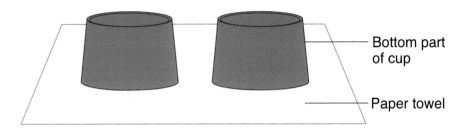

Bottom part
of cup

Paper towel

Figure 2

3. Allow the paint to dry.

4. Place 1 paper towel tube on its end, and with the pencil trace around the tube on a piece of light-gray construction paper (Figure 3).

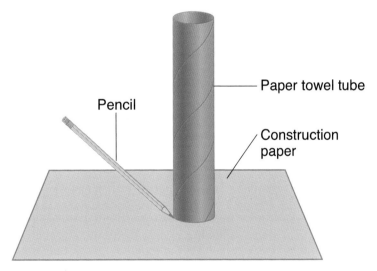

Pencil

Paper towel tube

Construction
paper

Figure 3

5. Repeat step 4.

6. Repeat step 4 again, now with the oatmeal container and a piece of dark-gray construction paper.

7. Cut all 3 resultant circles (the 2 light-gray smaller ones and the larger dark-gray one) in half (Figure 4).

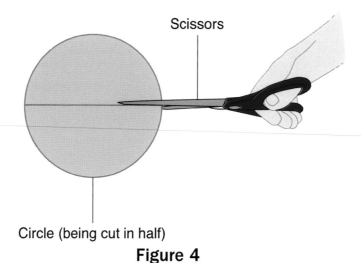

Scissors

Circle (being cut in half)

Figure 4

8. Fold 3 of the light-gray halves and 1 dark-gray half into cone shapes (Figure 5).

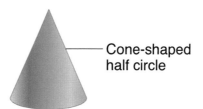

Cone-shaped
half circle

Figure 5

9. Glue the edges of the cones so that they do not come apart.

10. Glue the 2 painted cups to the inner portion of the bottoms of 2 of the cardboard paper towel tubes (Figure 6).

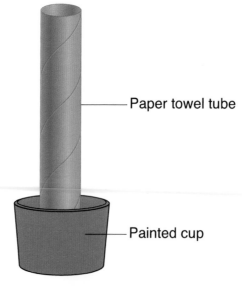

Paper towel tube

Painted cup

Figure 6

11. Add 2 dry beans to each of those cardboard tubes.

12. Using tape, attach a small cone to the top of each of those cardboard tubes (Figure 7).

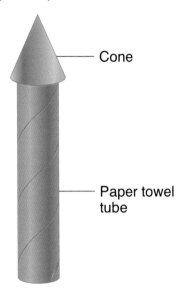

Cone

Paper towel tube

Figure 7

13. Repeat step 12 using the larger cone, and attach it to the oatmeal container.

14. Cover the cardboard tubes by gluing on light-gray construction paper, and then cover the oatmeal container with dark-gray construction paper.

15. Place the oatmeal container in between the 2 cardboard tubes you have covered, with the oatmeal container about 2 in. from the bottom of the tubes (Figure 8).

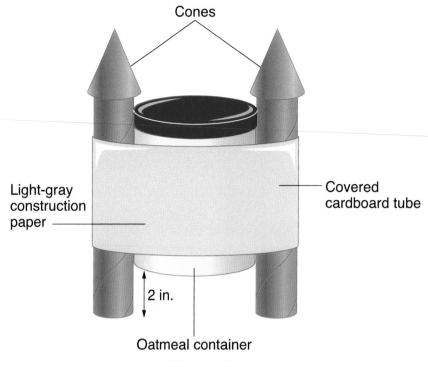

Figure 8

16. Glue the oatmeal container to the tubes.
17. Allow the glue to dry.
18. Cut out the space shuttle wings (Figure 9).

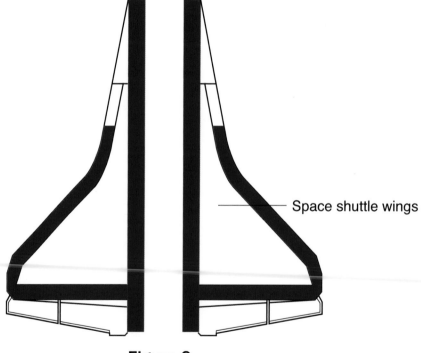

Figure 9

19. Cut out the tail sections and booster rockets (Figure 10).

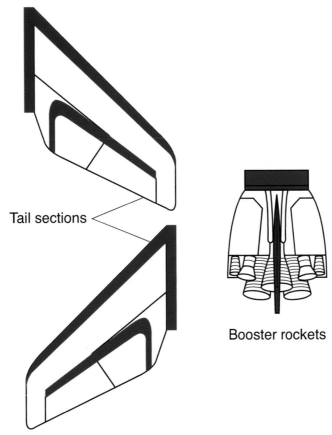

Figure 10

20. Cut 1 cardboard tube in half (Figure 11).

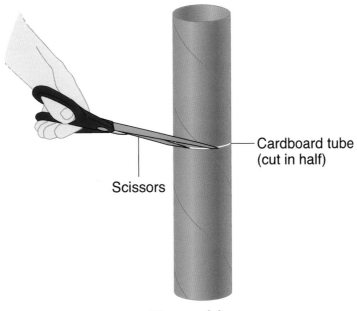

Figure 11

21. Cover the cardboard half-tube in light-gray construction paper, gluing the construction paper in place.

22. Glue the last gray cone to the top of the covered tube.

23. Glue the wing and tail sections to this tube (Figure 12).

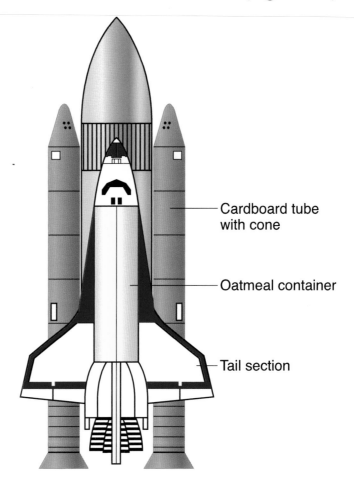

Cardboard tube with cone

Oatmeal container

Tail section

Figure 12

24. Glue your "shuttle" to the oatmeal container (which is the booster portion of the shuttle project) (Figure 12).

 **Observations**

1. Why did the model require the oatmeal container and extra cardboard tubes to be accurate? What purpose does the assembly simulate for the space shuttle?

2. Research the shuttle and write a short report that covers some or all of this information: When was the first shuttle mission? How many shuttles have been built? What are their names? What have the purposes been of their missions? Which astronauts have flown shuttle missions? What was unique about the shuttle compared to other rockets? What are the steps of the shuttle's flight path?

Our Findings

Please refer to the Our Findings appendix at the back of this volume.

Further Reading

Boyer, Paul S. "Space Program." *The Oxford Companion to United States History*. 2001. Accessed October 5, 2010. This article provides a brief overview of the United States space program.

Duggins, Pat. *Final Countdown: NASA and the End of the Space Shuttle Program*. Gainesville, FL: University Press of Florida, 2009. Well-written history of the shuttle program, including the effect of the *Columbia* tragedy on the decision to end the shuttle program permanently.

Jenkins, Dennis. *Space Shuttle: The History of the National Space Transportation System—The First 100 Missions*. Osceola, WI: Motorbooks International, 2001. Book includes photographs, schematics, and information for the space shuttle enthusiast.

"Sally K. Ride." *jsc.NASA.gov*. 2009. Available online. URL: http://www.jsc.nasa.gov/Bios/htmlbios/ride-sk.html. Accessed December 30, 2009. Biographical data about the first female American astronaut.

Simpson, Morgan. "NASA (National Air and Space Administration)." *Encyclopedia of Espionage, Intelligence, and Security*. 2004. Accessed October 5, 2010. Explains the history and purpose of NASA.

"Space Shuttle." NASA. 2009. Available online. URL: http://www.nasa.gov/mission_pages/shuttle/main/index.html. Accessed December 30, 2009. The official Web site of the space shuttle, including current information on upcoming launches.

"Space Shuttle." *The Columbia Encyclopedia*, 6th Edition. 2008. Accessed October 5, 2010. Article about the space shuttle missions of NASA.

"Space Shuttle Columbia Lost." *www.space.com*. 2003. Available online. URL: http://www.space.com/columbiatragedy/. Details and photographs of the tragic disaster of the shuttle *Columbia*, whose entire crew died.

20. USING ARCHES TO DESIGN AND CONSTRUCT A TUNNEL

Introduction

Arches are both *aesthetically* pleasing and important in the design of structures. Arches allow for heavy *loads* to be held without *collapsing*. For instance, many tunnels are built underground. The arches support the weight of the earth above the tunnel. In other words, arches support weight while *spanning* an area by reducing or eliminating *tensile stress*. Although arches were used as far back as ancient Mesopotamia, in Asia Minor, the Romans were among the first to utilize them for above-ground structures. Arches were used by the Romans for everything from bridges to large buildings. The Europeans later made variations of the arch.

The construction of an arch usually requires the building of an initial *frame*, typically wooden, which can be removed if the arch was built correctly around the frame. However, older buildings and structures with arches often need *reinforcement* as they age.

In this activity, you will create a model tunnel based on an arch design.

Time Needed

3 1/2 hours

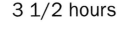

What You Need

- 9 large craft sticks (3/4 in. by 6 in.)
- hot tap water
- medium-sized bowl

- hot-glue gun
- glue for glue gun
- 1 unopened can of fruit or vegetables, 14 oz
- rubber bands
- sandpaper
- wire cutter
- acrylic craft paint
- stopwatch, timer, or clock

Safety Precautions

Please review and follow the safety guidelines at the beginning of this volume. Exercise caution when using hot-glue guns. Adult supervision is recommended.

What You Do

1. Fill the bowl with hot tap water.
2. Place 2 craft sticks into the hot water and allow them to soak for 30 minutes.
3. Remove the sticks from the water.
4. Carefully bend the craft sticks around the sides of the 14-oz can, and wrap 2 rubber bands around the can and sticks to secure them in place (Figure 1).

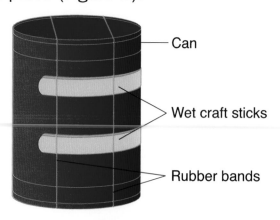

Figure 1

5. Place the can and sticks aside for 2 hours while the sticks dry.

6. Remove the now curved sticks from the can.

7. Using the hot-glue gun, glue the 2 curved sticks to a flat stick so that they do not go past the side of the stick (Figure 2). Make sure to keep all sticks aligned as much as possible.

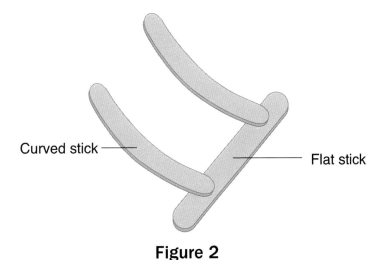

Curved stick   Flat stick

Figure 2

8. Keep gluing flat sticks onto the curved sticks, touching the sides of the flat sticks to the previous flat stick.

9. If necessary, use the wire cutter to cut the end of the curved sticks prior to gluing on the final straight stick if it seems that the curved sticks will extend past the side of the last flat stick (Figure 3). If you do cut the end, lightly sand the cut edges with sandpaper.

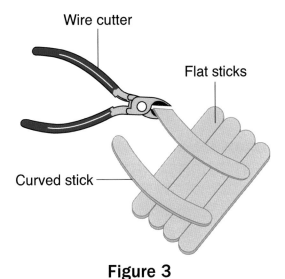

Wire cutter

Flat sticks

Curved stick

Figure 3

10. Stand up your creation. You have made a tunnel.

 **Observations**

1. What is the purpose of using an arch in the design of a tunnel?

2. Where else have you seen arches?

3. How do you think you might alter the design of this tunnel if you wanted to make it longer? Take into account what you would do to strengthen it in the middle if it was very long.

Our Findings

Please refer to the Our Findings appendix at the back of this volume.

Further Reading

"Arch." *The Columbia Encyclopedia*, 6th Edition. 2008. Accessed October 5, 2010. Explains the design and use of the arch in construction and architecture.

Donovan, Sandra. *The Channel Tunnel*. Minneapolis: Lerner Publication, 2003. Young-adult book that details the construction of the English Channel; includes illustrations and photos.

"Glossary: All About Arches." *Curvemakers.com*. Available online. URL: http://www.curvemakers.com/about_arches.html. Accessed December 21, 2009. Diagrams, photographs, and explanations of every type of arch used in building design.

Hancock, Paul, and Brian J. Skinner. "Tunnels." *The Oxford Companion to the Earth*. 2000. Accessed October 5, 2010. Overview of the history of tunnels.

Oxlade, Chris. *Tunnels*. Chicago: Heinemann-Raintree, 2005. Children's book exploring the engineering used in the creation of tunnels.

"Roman Arches." *Hadrians.com*. Available online. URL: //www. hadrians.com/rome/romans/sources/roman_arches.html. Accessed December 21, 2009. Web site that explains the Romans' use of arches in building; includes diagrams of arches.

Strickland, Carol. *The Annotated Arch: A Crash Course in the History of Architecture.* Riverside, NJ: Andrew McMeel Publishing, 2001. A dynamic book about architecture with succinct explanations and historical background information.

"The Theatre at Aspendos, Turkey." *The Ancient Theater Archive.* Available online. URL: http://www.whitman.edu/theatre/theatretour/ aspendos/introduction/aspendos.intro2.htm. Accessed December 21, 2009. Detailed history and description of architecture in theaters of ancient Rome and Turkey.

"Tunnel." *The Columbia Encyclopedia*, 6th Edition. 2008. October 5, 2010. Overview of the design and construction of tunnels.

Scope and Sequence Chart

This chart is aligned with the National Science Content Standards. Each state may have its own specific content standards, so please refer to your local and state content standards for additional information. As always, adult supervision is recommended (or required in some instances), and discretion should be used in selecting experiments appropriate for each age group or individual children.

Standard	Experiments
Unifying Concepts and Processes	all
Science as Inquiry	all
Physical Science	
Properties of objects and materials	2, 3, 4, 5, 8, 10, 11, 17, 20
Properties and changes of properties in matter	
Position and motion of objects	2, 4, 5, 9, 12, 13, 14, 16, 18, 19
Motions and forces	2, 3, 4, 5, 6, 7, 9, 12, 13, 14, 16, 18, 19
Light, heat, electricity, and magnetism	7, 12, 14, 17, 18
Transfer of energy	2, 4, 7, 9, 12, 13, 14, 19
Life Science	
Structure and function in living systems	
Life cycles of organisms	
Reproduction and heredity	
Regulation and behavior	
Organisms and environments	

Populations and ecosystems	
Diversity and adaptations of organisms	
Earth Science	
Properties of Earth materials	
Structure of the Earth system	6
Objects in the sky	6, 19
Changes in Earth and sky	
Earth's history	
Earth in the solar system	
Science and Technology	all
Science in Personal and Social Perspectives	
Personal health	
Characteristics and changes in populations	
Types of resources	7, 10, 12, 13, 17
Changes in environments	7
Science and technology in local challenges	1, 3, 4, 7, 8, 10, 11, 12, 13, 15, 16, 17, 18, 20
Populations, resources, and environments	7, 12, 13, 17
Natural hazards	4
Risks and benefits	7
Science and technology in society	1, 3, 4, 5, 7, 8, 9, 10, 12, 13, 14, 15, 16, 18, 19, 20
History and Nature of Science	all

Grade Level

Title of Experiment	Grade Level
1. Investigating What Engineers Do	5–8
2. Building a Launcher/Catapult	5–8
3. Building and Testing a Suspension Bridge	5–8
4. Building an Earthquake-Proof Structure	5–8
5. Designing a Parachute	5–8
6. Demonstrating Satellite Orbits	5–8
7. Building a Working-Model Dam	5–8
8. Modeling "Asphalt"	5–8
9. Creating a Full-Size Hovercraft	5–8
10. Testing the Durability of Different Building Materials	5–8
11. Testing the Effectiveness of Sound Barriers	5–8
12. Making a Windmill	5–8
13. Making a Waterwheel	5–8
14. Designing a Rube Goldberg Machine	5–8
15. Building a Model Skyscraper	5–8
16. Constructing a Skateboard Ramp	5–8
17. Building an Igloo	5–8
18. Making a Door Alarm	5–8
19. Investigating and Making a Model of the Space Shuttle	5–8
20. Using Arches to Design and Construct a Tunnel	5–8

Setting

The experiments are classified by materials and equipment use as follows:

- Those under SCHOOL LABORATORY involve materials and equipment found only in science laboratories. Those under SCHOOL LABORATORY must be carried out there under the supervision of the teacher or another adult.

- Those under HOME involve household or everyday materials. Some of these can be done at home, but call for supervision.

- The experiments classified under OUTDOORS may be done at the school or at the home, but require access to outdoor areas and call for supervision.

SCHOOL LABORATORY

9. Creating a Full-Size Hovercraft

HOME

1. Investigating What Engineers Do
2. Building a Launcher/Catapult
3. Building and Testing a Suspension Bridge
4. Building an Earthquake-Proof Structure
6. Demonstrating Satellite Orbits
7. Building a Working-Model Dam
8. Modeling "Asphalt"
10. Testing the Durability of Different Building Materials
11. Testing the Effectiveness of Sound Barriers
12. Making a Windmill
13. Making a Waterwheel
14. Designing a Rube Goldberg Machine

OUTDOORS

Our Findings

1. INVESTIGATING WHAT ENGINEERS DO

1. Answers will vary.

2. Answers will vary.

3. Answers will vary.

2. BUILDING A LAUNCHER/CATAPULT

1. Answers will vary.

2. Answers will vary.

3. The device is based on the lever.

4. Answers will vary.

3. BUILDING AND TESTING A SUSPENSION BRIDGE

1. Answers will vary.

2. Answers will vary.

3. The suspension bridge will hold more weight because the tension in the strings offsets some of the weight and stress placed on the bridge.

4. Answers will vary but may include providing more support by adding more suspension points.

4. MAKING AN EARTHQUAKE-PROOF STRUCTURE

1. Answers will vary.

2. Answers will vary.

3. Engineers can design buildings that will remain standing in case of an earthquake, protecting the people inside and near the building and preventing (or reducing) the loss of life/risk of injury.

4. Answers will vary but may include blending with the surroundings, beauty, functionality.

5. DESIGNING A PARACHUTE

1. Answers will vary but will most likely be the smallest one.

2. Answers will vary but will most likely be the largest one.

3. Parachutes fall because of the pull of gravity.

4. The relationship is as follows: the larger the surface area, the longer the time for the parachute to fall.

6. DEMONSTRATING SATELLITE ORBITS

1. Answers will vary, but most likely the steeper the angle, the faster the object moved.

2. The baseball represented the Sun, the golf ball represented a large planet, and the marble represented a small planet. Another possible answer is that the baseball represented the Earth and either the golf ball or marble represented the Moon.

3. Objects travel at different rates around the Sun depending on mass and distance from the Sun.

7. BUILDING A WORKING-MODEL DAM

1. The water will shoot out the furthest at the highest marking.

2. The farther the water is spouting, the higher the water pressure.

3. Dams are built wider at the bottom to handle the additional water pressure and force sustained on the dam lower down.

4. Answers will vary.

8. MODELING "ASPHALT"

1. The ingredients listed in "What you Need" each represents items used in making actual asphalt.

2. Just as in actual asphalt (sometimes mistakenly referred to as tar), a thick, hot, molten liquid holds together the other aggregates. Both asphalt and chocolate harden when dry.

3. Paving roads is typically supervised by civil engineers. Examples will vary but may include building bridges and tunnels.

9. CREATING A FULL-SIZE HOVERCRAFT

1. The leaf blower is serving as the engine.

2. The plastic sheet serves as the skirt.

3. Air is generated beneath the craft, lifting the hovercraft off the surface on which it sits. The craft can then move on the cushion of air.

4. The hair blower would not generate enough power to lift the hovercraft.

5. Answers will vary.

10. TESTING THE DURABILITY OF DIFFERENT BUILDING MATERIALS

1. Answers will vary.

2. Answers will vary.

3. Answers will vary.

4. Answers will vary but may include: no, they do not always have to sustain weight or force. Some might be decorative in nature.

11. TESTING THE EFFECTIVENESS OF SOUND BARRIERS

1. Answers will vary but should be yes, there was a difference.

2. Answers will vary.

3. Yes, answers will vary.

4. Sound barriers are constructed near highways to reduce the traffic noise and noise pollution experienced by local residents and nearby businesses.

5. Answers will vary.

12. MAKING A WINDMILL

1. Answers will vary.

2. Answers will vary.

3. Answers will vary but may include generating electricity.

13. MAKING A WATERWHEEL

1. The waterwheel turned when the water was turned on.

2. The bucket was raised when the water was turned on.

3. Answers will vary.

4. They were used to generate power and move items so that people would not have to exert that force.

14. DESIGNING A RUBE GOLDBERG MACHINE

1. No, if done correctly, the device was not the simplest way to complete the task. That is the point of a Rube Goldberg machine.

2. Answers will vary.

3. Answers will vary.

4. Answers will vary.

15. BUILDING A MODEL SKYSCRAPER

1. Answers will vary.

2. Answers will vary.

3. Answers will vary.

4. Answers will vary.

16. CONSTRUCTING A SKATEBOARD RAMP

1. When going down a ramp, the pull of gravity will cause deceleration; by the same token, when going up a ramp, the friction from the ramp and the pull downwards of gravity will slow a skater.

2. Answers will vary but may include: Make the ramp steeper or longer.

3. Actually, this is called a halfpipe; it allows skaters to accelerate and decelerate, go back and forth, and do tricks.

4. Answers will vary.

17. BUILDING AN IGLOO

1. Understanding how domes are built and how their weight is supported is vital for constructing an igloo that will not collapse.

2. Igloos are made of ice, so they can only be temporary since ice melts and/or changes shape over time because of variations in temperature.

3. Answers will vary but may include: sugar cubes, cardboard, clay, and Styrofoam.™

4. Larger domed buildings exist and could be built based on this type of engineering. Also, the use of ice in construction has become well known; it was used to build the famous Ice Hotel in Sweden.

18. MAKING A DOOR ALARM

1. When the cardboard is removed, the circuit is completed and the electricity flows to the buzzer, making it sound.

2. Answers will vary.

3. Answers will vary.

4. Answers will vary but may include: This technology can be used to create simple security devices and buzzers for other uses.

19. INVESTIGATING AND MAKING A MODEL OF THE SPACE SHUTTLE

1. These items represent the booster rockets needed to initially launch the shuttle into space.

2. Answers will vary.

20. USING ARCHES TO DESIGN AND CONSTRUCT A TUNNEL

1. The arches support the weight of the earth above the tunnel.

2. Answers will vary.

3. Answers will vary.

Tips for Teachers

General
- Always review all safety guidelines before attempting any experiment.
- Enforce all safety guidelines.
- Try the experiment on your own first to be better prepared for possible questions that may arise.
- You may try demonstrating each step of the experiment as you explain it to the students.
- Check for correlation to standards in order to best match the experiment to the curriculum.
- Provide adult assistance and supervision. Do not leave students unsupervised.
- Make sure students feel comfortable asking for help when needed.

Equipment and Supplies
- Most glassware can be purchased from scientific supply companies like Carolina Science Supply Company. Many companies have both print and online catalogs.
- Chemicals and special materials can also be purchased from these companies.
- Many of the supplies and substances used in the experiments are household items that can be found at home or purchased at a local market.
- For some of the hard-to-find items (e.g., extra-large jars), try asking local restaurants, or check warehouse-type stores that carry industrial-size items. For some substances (e.g., lamp oil), you should check with hardware or home-improvement stores.

Special-Needs Students
- Please make sure to follow the individualized education plans (IEPs) and 504 accommodation plans for any special-needs students who have them.
- Provide a handout for students who require visual aids.
- Create a graphic representation of the experiment for students who use picture cards to communicate.
- For visually disabled students, provide copies with enlarged print.
- Involve students with dexterity issues by providing opportunities to participate in ways that match their abilities—e.g., be the timekeeper or the instruction reader.
- Read aloud directions for students who require verbal cues.

(continued)

- Record the instructions for playback.
- Repeat instructions more than once.
- Demonstrate the experiment so that students can see how it should be done correctly.
- Check frequently for comprehension.
- Ask students to repeat the information so that you can ensure accuracy.
- Break down directions into simple steps.
- Have students work with a lab partner or in a lab group.
- Provide adult assistance when necessary.
- Make sure that students with auditory disabilities know visual cues in case of danger or emergency.
- Simplify the experiment for students with developmental disabilities.
- Incorporate assistive technology for students who require it; e.g., use of Alphasmart® keyboards for recording observations and for dictation software.
- Provide preferred seating (e.g., front row) for students with disabilities to ensure they are able to see and hear demonstrations.
- Provide an interpreter if available for students with auditory disabilities who require American Sign Language.
- Consult with your school's inclusion specialist, resource teacher, or special education teacher for additional suggestions.
- Arrange furniture so that all students have clear access to information being presented and can move about the room (e.g., wheelchair-accessible aisles of about 48 inches).
- Offer students the option of recording their responses.
- Eliminate background noise when it is distracting.
- Face the class when speaking, and keep your face visible for students who lip-read.
- Repeat new words in various contexts to enhance vocabulary.
- Alter table heights for wheelchair access.
- Substitute equipment with larger sizes for easy gripping.
- Ask the student if he or she needs help before offering it.
- Place materials within easy reach of the students.
- Be aware of temperature. Some students may not be able to feel heat or cold and might injure themselves.
- Identify yourself to students with visual impairments. Also speak when you enter or leave the room.
- For visually impaired students, give directions in relation to the student's body. Do not use words like "over here." Also describe verbally what is happening in the experiment.

Glossary

A

absorption	taking in or incorporation of something
acoustical engineering	branch of engineering dealing with sound and vibration
acoustics	scientific study of sound
adhesive	substance that causes two surfaces to stick together
advent	arrival of something extremely important
aerospace	relating to the science and technology of flight and space travel
aesthetically	concerning the appreciation of beauty or good taste; artistic
aesthetics	an idea of what is artistically valid or beautiful
aggregates	mineral materials, such as sand or stone
amphibious	combining two qualities, such as being able to live on both land and water
amplitude	the height of the crest, or the depth of the trough, of a wave
anchored	fixed or fastened
aqueducts	pipe or channel designed to transport water from a remote source, usually by gravity
arch	a structure having a curved appearance
arch dams	a thin, curved structure built to curve upstream so that the force of the water against it squeezes the arch, compressing and strengthening the structure and pushing it into the ground
artillery	mounted projectile-firing guns; missile launchers
asphalt	a thick, sticky, dark-brown mixture of petroleum tars used in paving, roofing, and waterproofing; a petroleum by-product
asphaltum	term used for asphalt found in natural deposits
astronomer	a scientist who studies the universe beyond the Earth; a stargazer
attributed	resulting from a known cause
axis	the line about which a rotating body, such as the Earth, turns
axle	the central region for a rotating wheel or gear

B

barriers	boundaries, or limits; obstacles

binder   a substance for holding loose material together

booster rockets   large solid rockets used by the space shuttle during the first 2
                        minutes of powered flight

budget   the total sum of money set aside or needed for a purpose

C

cables   cords of metal wire used to support, operate, or pull a mechanism

calcium nitrate   colorless crystals used in explosives; $Ca(NO_3)_2$

cargo bay   the large central area of the space shuttle which carries the instruments
                        and equipment for an aircraft or spacecraft

cartoonist   someone who draws cartoons, or comic strips

catapult   a machine used to launch projectiles

ceramic   pertaining to products made from clay and similar materials

check dams   small barriers built across the direction of water flow on shallow rivers
                        and streams for the purpose of water harvesting

civil engineering   the branch of engineering that specializes in the design and construction
                        of structures such as bridges, roads, and dams

climate   a region's usual weather patterns

coarseness   harsh or grating quality

cofferdam   temporary watertight enclosure that is pumped dry to expose the bottom
                        of a body of water so that construction may ensue

collapsing   falling together or inward; crumbling

compression   force that tends to shorten or squeeze something, decreasing its
                        volume

compression waves   a wave in which the particles are close together

concave   curved inward, like the inside of a circle or sphere

concrete   an artificial, stone-like material used for various structural purposes

construction   the industry of building

contraptions   mechanical devices

cost-effective   the best quality for the least amount of money

cruciform   having the shape of a cross

D

dam   a barrier to block or control the flow of water

decibels (dB)   unit of measurement of the volume of sound

descent   falling or sinking

device	a thing made for a particular purpose; an invention
diversionary dam	a dam that diverts all or a portion of the flow of a river from its natural course
drag	the force acting on a moving object, opposite in direction to the movement of the object, as it passes through air or water
durability	ability to resist decay
dwelling	living

E

earthquake	a shaking of the surface of the Earth caused by the release of stress along geologic faults or by volcanic activity
electrical	branch of engineering that specializes in the design, construction, and practical uses of electrical systems
electricity	flow of electrical charges through a conductor
electromagnetism	magnetism produced by electric charge in motion
ellipse	a closed, symmetric curve shaped like an oval
elliptical	oval-shaped
embankment dams	massive dams made of earth and rock
engineer	(verb) to design or create with machines; or (noun) one who does so
engineering	application of science to practical uses such as the design of structures, machines, and systems
epicycles	a circle that rolls, externally or internally, on another circle
erosion	type of weathering in which surface soil and rock are worn away through the action of glaciers, water, and wind
external	toward the outside; outer

F

feat	a notable act of skill, or strength; an achievement
fixed horizontal-axle windmills	windmills oriented to the prevailing wind (see also **horizontal-axle windmills**)
force	strength or power exerted on an object
foundation	the basis on which a thing stands or is supported
frame	a structure that gives shape or support
frequency	the rate at which a repeating event occurs, such as the cycle of a wave
friction	rubbing of the surface of one body against that of another

G

gas   substance possessing the property of indefinite expansion; or a
                           combustible fluid used as fuel, such as natural gas

gears   wheels with teeth around their rims that mesh with the teeth of other
                           wheels to transmit motion

gravitational   relating to the force of attraction between any two masses

gravity dam   a dam resisting the pressure of impounded water through its own weight

grenades   small bombs or explosive missiles that are detonated by a fuse and
                           thrown by hand or shot from a rifle or launcher

grinding mills   mills designed to break a solid material into smaller pieces

H

halfpipe   U-shaped ramp used by snowboarders and skateboarders to provide
                           a takeoff for a jump

harness   (verb) to gain control over for effective use

horizontal-axle   mills designed to rotate with the prevailing wind, for use in such places
  windmills   as Northwestern Europe, where wind directions vary (see also **fixed
                           horizontal-axle windmills**)

hovercraft   a vehicle designed for traveling over land or water, supported by a cushion
                           of slowly moving, low-pressure air

hulls   the outer casings of a rocket, guided missile, or spaceship

hydroelectric plants   power facilities that harness the energy produced by flowing water

                           and use simple machines to convert the energy into electricity

I

igloo (iglu)   an Eskimo house, being a dome-shaped hut usually built of blocks of
                           hard snow

infrastructure   the basic, underlying framework of a system or organization

Inuit   a member of the Eskimo peoples inhabiting northernmost North America
                           from northern Alaska to eastern Canada and Greenland

irrigation   the artificial application of water to land to sustain growing plants

L

liquid   a phase of matter in which atoms or molecules can move freely while
                           remaining in contact with one another; a liquid takes the shape of its
                           container

load   a weight or mass that is supported or carried

longitudinal waves   a wave that oscillates back and forth on an axis that is the same as the axis along which the wave moves; for example, sound waves

lubricate   to make slippery or smooth, as to reduce friction

M

maneuvers   controlled changes in movement or direction of a moving vehicle or vessel, as in the flight path of an aircraft

manufacture   to make or produce by hand or machinery

masonry   stonework or brickwork

medieval   a descriptive term for people, objects, events, and institutions of the Middle Ages

mill   a building or collection of buildings that has machinery for manufacture; a factory

mortar   any of various materials or compounds for bonding together bricks, stones, etc.

mummification   the process by which the body of a human or animal is embalmed and prepared for burial; custom of ancient Egyptians

N

noise pollution   environmental noise that is annoying, distracting, or physically harmful

O

orbit   path followed by an object revolving around another object, under the influence of gravity

orbital vehicle   a craft or machine designed to enter a closed orbit around the Earth or around other celestial bodies

P

paper mills   a factory devoted to making paper from wood pulp

parachute   a fabric device used to float down safely after free falling from an aircraft

parafoils   structures, usually made of a strong, light fabric, having a shape similar to that of an airplane wing; used as a kite or a parachute

patent   government license that gives the holder exclusive rights to a process, design, or new invention for a designated period of time

pave   to prepare a pathway so that it is smooth and safe to travel on

paver   a person or thing that paves

payload   passengers, crew, instruments, or equipment carried by an aircraft, spacecraft, or rocket

period   the duration of one complete cycle of a wave or oscillation

physician   doctor of medicine (M.D.)

physicist   scientist who specializes in matter and energy, and of the interactions between the two

pillar   a vertical support; a column

projectiles   a fired, thrown, or otherwise propelled object, such as a bullet, having no capacity for self-propulsion

propel   to cause to move forward

prototype   an original, full-scale, and usually working model of a new product or new version of an existing product

Q

quarter pipe   a ramp used in extreme sports resembling one-fourth the cross section of a cylindrical pipe

R

radar   a method of finding the position and velocity of an object by bouncing a radio wave off it and analyzing the reflected wave

ram-air parachutes self-inflating parachutes that provide control of speed and direction similar to that of paragliders

recycled   used again, especially to reprocess

reflection   a bouncing of something, as in light or sound, off a surface

reinforcement   something that strengthens, as in a system of steel bars, strands, wires, or mesh for absorbing the tensile and shearing stresses in concrete work

renaissance   cultural rebirth that occurred in Europe from roughly the 14th through the middle of the 17th centuries, based on the rediscovery of the literature of Greece and Rome

renewable resource any resource, such as wood or solar energy, that can or will be replenished naturally in the course of time

reservoir   natural or artificial pond or lake used for the storage and regulation of water

resistant   opposed to something

S

saddle dams   an auxiliary dam constructed by a primary dam either to permit a higher water elevation and storage or to limit the extent of a reservoir for increased efficiency

sawmills   a facility where logs are cut into boards

sea carriers	large vessels for transporting materials over vast bodies of water
shale	sedimentary rock formed from layers of clay
shelter	something that provides cover or protection, as from the weather
sieges	the acts or processes of surrounding and attacking a fortified place in such a way as to isolate it from help and supplies
simple machines	devices that transmit or modify force or motion; any of six or more elementary mechanisms, as the lever, wheel and axle, pulley, screw, wedge, and inclined plane
skirt	curtain around a base
skyline	the outline of something, as the buildings of a city, against the sky
skyscrapers	relatively tall buildings, usually for office or commercial use
solid	a substance having a definite shape and volume; one that is neither liquid nor gaseous
sonic	pertaining to a speed equal to that of sound in air
sound	vibrations capable of being detected by human organs of hearing
space shuttle	a reusable spacecraft with wings, designed to transport astronauts between Earth and an orbiting space station and also used to deploy and retrieve satellites
span	the full extent, stretch, or reach of anything, as in airplane wings
structure	something built or constructed, as a building, bridge, or dam
surpassed	to go beyond in excellence or achievement; be superior to
suspension bridge	a bridge having a deck suspended from cables anchored at their ends and usually raised on towers

T

technology	the specific methods, materials, and devices used to solve practical problems, especially for industrial or commercial objectives
tensile stress	stress that tends to cause something to become longer along the direction of applied force, thus weakening the material
tension	force that tends to stretch or elongate something
terrain	surface features of an area of land
timber dam	a dam that uses wood, often in the form of sticks and branches, with a relatively short lifespan; rarely used today
tornadoes	violently destructive windstorms that move in funnel-shaped columns, made visible by condensation and debris
transverse wave	a wave that oscillates perpendicular to the axis along which the wave travels, as in electromagnetic waves or waves in bodies of water

V

vacuum space empty of matter

vehicle device or structure for transporting people or things

velocity the speed and direction of motion of a moving body

vertical-axle windmills made of 6 to 12 sails covered in reed matting or cloth material, these machines were used to grind corn or draw water

vibrations rapid movements of a particle, particles, or elastic solid or surface, back and forth across a central position

viscous having relatively high resistance to flow; sticky

W

water pressure the force that results from the weight of water overhead

waterwheel a wheel propelled by falling or running water and used to power machinery

wave a disturbance traveling through a medium by which energy is transferred from one particle of the medium to another without causing any permanent displacement of the medium itself

wavelength the distance between crests (or troughs) of a wave

windmills any of various machines for grinding, pumping, etc., driven by the force of the wind acting on a number of vanes or sails

Internet Resources

The Internet is a wealth of information and resources for students, parents, and teachers. However, all sources should be verified for fact, and it is recommended never to rely on any single source for in-depth research. The following list of resources is a sample of what the World Wide Web has to offer. The sites listed were accessible as of December 2010.

Aerospaceweb.org. "What Does an Aerospace Engineer Do?" Available online. URL: http://www.aerospaceweb.org/question/careers/q0018.shtml. Accessed October 5, 2010. Discusses the jobs that aerospace engineers do.

Bellis, Mary. "Hovercraft." Available online. URL: http://inventors.about.com/library/inventors/blhovercraft.htm. Accessed November 20, 2009. Gives background on hovercrafts and links on building them.

Bergen County Technical Schools. "Hair Analysis." Available online. URL: http://sites.bergen.org/forensic/HairAnalysis.htm. Accessed July 16, 2009. Detailed explanation of slide preparation for hair analysis.

California State University Long Beach. "What Do Engineers Do?" Available online. URL: http://www.csulb.edu/colleges/coe/views/choosing/engineers.shtml. Accessed October 5, 2010. Web site of CSULB's engineering department.

The Chemistry Detectives. "Developing Fingerprints." Available online. URL: http://www.chm.bris.ac.uk/webprojects2002/thomson/fingerprints2.htm. Accessed July 17, 2009. Provides information on how to develop fingerprints.

Cheresources. Available online. URL: http://www.cheresources.com/questions/experimentation_and_testing-136.html. Accessed July 16, 2009. Discusses methods of analyzing powders.

Clark, Jim. "Flame Tests." Available online. URL: http://www.chemguide.co.uk/inorganic/group1/flametests.html. Accessed July 18, 2009. Guide to conducting flame tests.

Ekman, Dr. Paul. Available online. URL: http://www.paulekman.com/micros/. Accessed July 20, 2009. Web site about the lie expert about whom the television show *Lie to Me* is based.

Electronic Circuits. "Simple Lie Detector." Available online. URL: http://www. aaroncake.net/circuits/lie.asp?showcomments=all. Accessed July 20, 2009. Schematics for building a simple, working lie detector.

Encyclopedia of Surgery. "Urinalysis." Available online. URL: http://www. surgeryencyclopedia.com/St-Wr/Urinalysis.html. Accessed July 13, 2009. Provides definition and uses of urinalysis.

Engineeringedge.com. "What Do Mechanical Engineers Do?" Available online. URL: http://www.engineersedge.com/mechanical_engineering/what_do_mechanical_ engineers_do.htm. Accessed October 5, 2010. Explanation of what a mechanical engineer does on a daily basis.

Forensic Science Communications. "Collection, Handling, and Identification of Glass." Available online. URL: http://www.fbi.gov/hq/lab/fsc/backissu/jan2005/ standards/2005standards5.htm. Accessed July 14, 2009. Explains how forensic experts should handle glass objects for analysis.

History of Fingerprints, A. "Diagnosis Crime." Available online. URL: http:// diagnosiscrime.wordpress.com/2008/04/25/a-history-of-fingerprints/. Accessed July 14, 2009. Provides an excellent detailed history on how fingerprints came to be used for identification.

"How to Detect Lies." Blifaloo.com. Available online. URL: http://www.blifaloo.com/ info/lies.php. Accessed July 20, 2009. Provides a short "how to" lesson on reading faces.

James, Cullen. "Veteran Recalls Navajo Code Talkers' War in the Pacific." Available online. URL: http://www.defenselink.mil/news/newsarticle.aspx?id=43012. Accessed July 14, 2009. Article about how Navajos created and deciphered codes during wartime.

Joseph, Linda. "Adventures of Cyberbee." Available online. URL: http://www.cyberbee. com. Accessed July 16, 2009. Contains links to educational resources in various fields of study.

Life Training Online. "How to Read People." Available online. URL: http://www. lifetrainingonline.com/blog/how-to-detect-lies.htm. Accessed July 20, 2009. Blog with helpful tips and links related to lie detecting.

Michigan State University. "What Do Engineers Do?" Available online. URL: http://www.egr.msu.edu/future-engineer/what. Accessed October 5, 2010. Web site from the engineering department of Michigan State University explaining the types of jobs that engineers perform.

Nabili, Siamak, MD, MPH. "Urinalysis." Available online. URL: http://www.medicinenet.com/urinalysis/article.htm. Accessed July 13, 2009. Explains the process and purpose of urinalysis.

Science Made Simple. "Autumn Leaf Color." Available online. URL: http://www.sciencemadesimple.com/leaves.html. Accessed November 20, 2009. Explains why leaves turn colors with the seasons and provides simple activities related to the topic.

Shodor. "A History of Fingerprints." Available online. URL: http://shodor.org. Accessed July 14, 2009. Recounts the detailed history of how fingerprints came to be studied and used in crime solving and identification.

"Uncertainty Analysis in Forensic Science." *World of Forensic Science*. Thomson Gale, 2005. Encyclopedia.com. Available online. URL: http://www.encyclopedia.com/doc/1G2-3448300579.html. Accessed November 18, 2009. Discusses items to be taken into account during analyses of evidence.

University of New Mexico. "What is Civil Engineering?" Available online. URL: http://www.unm.edu/~%20civil/whatcivil.html. Accessed October 5, 2010. Explains what a civil engineer does and the courses for obtaining a degree in civil engineering.

Walsh, Dennis, Andra Renzi, and Sherri Aruda. "In the Lab: Attempting to identify gender and age through urinalysis screening." *Forensic Magazine*. Available online. URL: http://www.forensicmag.com/newsletters/features/newsletter_urinalysis01172007.html. Accessed July 13, 2009. Short explanation of how urinalysis can be used to identify factors.

Worldwidelearn.com. "Guide to College Majors in Industrial Engineering." Available online. URL: http://www.worldwidelearn.com/online-education-guide/engineering/industrial-engineering-major.htm. Accessed October 5, 2010. Explains industrial engineering and what coursework is necessary to obtain a degree in industrial engineering.

Index